Metaphor and myth in science and religion

Earl R. MacCormac

Metaphor and myth in science and religion

Duke University Press

Durham, North Carolina   1976

© 1976, Duke University Press
L.C.C. card no. 75–23941
I.S.B.N. 0–8223–0347–7
Printed in the United
States of America

Contents

Preface

This study was originally begun with two major purposes in mind: (1) an investigation of the use of metaphor by scientists and theologians; and (2) an assessment of the philosophical demands for meaning placed upon religious language. The two aims united in a single theme when I found that scientific language employed metaphors in a manner similar to the religious uses of metaphor, so that to object to religion because its nonliteral language failed to meet a philosophical criterion for meaning such as falsifiability, without also faulting science for the same reason, commits an act of the greatest hypocrisy. Spurred on by the discovery, I then sought to construct a theory of metaphor that would account not only for scientific and religious uses, but also for literary and philosophical uses. Although this study examines religious and scientific metaphors, I believe that the theory of metaphor presented can apply to most other uses. My theory begins with the "tension theory" of metaphor constructed in the past twenty years by a combination of literary critics and philosophers and modifies it by recasting the notion of metaphor as a process instead of leaving the term as a static category of classification. Some of the early results of my study of scientific and religious metaphors and my proposal for a theory of metaphor have been reported in a number of articles including: "Meaning Variance and Metaphor," *British Journal for the Philosophy of Science*, 22 (1971), 145–159; "Metaphor Revisited," *The Journal of Aesthetics and Art Criticism*, 30 (Winter, 1971), 239–250; "Metaphor and Literature," *The Journal of Aesthetic Education*, 6, no. 3 (July, 1972), 57–70; "The Language Machine and Metaphor," *Philosophy of the Social Sciences*, 2 (1972), 277–289; and "Scientific and Religious Metaphors," *Religious Studies*, forthcoming. The present volume does not constitute an anthology of these articles, but extends ideas and arguments set forth in them.

One piece of serendipity arising from the study of metaphor was the extension into a concurrent theory of myth. The interpretation of myth as the false attribution of reality to a suggestive metaphor, however, forced me to struggle with the realization that scientists as well as theologians have formulated myths. Great was my surprise at this unexpected turn of events since I had always thought of myths as the province of literature and religion with contemporary science free from such contamination. As I looked at the the history of science, I began to realize that many discarded scientific theories were just as mythical in the sense that they were *believed to be actual accounts of reality* as religious stories about the gods and their creation of the world.

At the end of this study, I make a few speculative suggestions about the nature of explanation applicable to both science and religion. These general remarks should be taken as no more than just that, speculations, because to engage in an investigation of a common theory of knowledge goes far beyond the intended scope of this study.

Many colleagues and friends have influenced my thought on metaphor and I am indebted to them for their assistance. Professor Raymond Martin of the Department of Philosophy of the University of Maryland and Professor Donald T. Campbell of the Department of Psychology of Northwestern University read earlier versions of this manuscript and offered helpful suggestions for improvement. Over a period of years, I had extensive conversations about language and metaphor with my former colleague, Dr. Alan B. Brinkley, and his insights and challenges are deeply appreciated. I want also to acknowledge the friendship and encouragement that I have received from Dr. George L. Abernethy, Dana Professor of Philosophy at Davidson College. Generous support for this research was provided by the Faculty Research Fund of Davidson College. Mrs. Nancy Blackwell typed the final manuscript and Mrs. Jean Daughtry, my present secretary, kindly typed a number of revisions. My deepest gratitude goes to my wife, Nancy, who offered constant encouragement and to whom this book is dedicated.

Introduction

Many contemporary philosophers firmly believe that religious language suffers from the fatal disease of meaninglessness. Judged by the criterion for meaning of verifiability or falsifiability that positivists employed, religious discourse was indicted as untestable. Critics also objected to the imprecise, vague, and ambiguous terms often used by theologians. And the large number of metaphors appearing in religious language epitomized these faults. How could one understand theological language as meaningful when it was shot through with metaphors and myths that seemed to defy empirical confirmation? Religious apologists attempted to deny these charges by presenting defenses that demonstrated that religious language could be confirmed by unusual means like finding confirmation through religious experience or expecting it in life after death. These debates about whether religious language could be justified as meaningful became tortured, in that theologians were convinced that they were uttering language that was *in fact* understood by not only themselves, but also by critics. Yet, they also found it difficult, if not impossible, to present the kind of apology that would satisfy criticial philosophers. This failure led some theologians to abandon any effort at a defense at all. They claimed that religious language was different from other languages that could fulfill these criteria for meaning. They assumed that religious lanaguage possessed a criterion for meaning of its own and that to test it by a criterion foreign to it was illegitimate. And the work of Wittgenstein in his *Philosophical Investigations* provided reinforcement for the view that there were various languages each possessing its own linguistic rules by which it could be understood.

At the same time that religious language was indicted for meaninglessness, scientific language was upheld as the epitome of proper meaningful language. Many of the same philosophers who faulted religious discourse as untestable, ambiguous, imprecise, and vague also believed that the language of scientists was confirmable, unambiguous, precise, and clear. Recent developments in the philosophy of science, however, have shown that the early hopes held out by positivists for scientific language as an empirically testable language were doomed to failure. Relatively few scientific statements can be tested directly in the empirical world, and even when negative evidence appears, as it often does, it is not clear just what constituent parts of a theory have been falsified. Positivists had hoped that theoretical terms that were not testable could be reduced by logical relations to observation statements. This program also failed, for there are numerous terms that cannot be so reduced and the very logical procedures used in reduction do not necessarily prevent the introduction of nonscientific terms, metaphysical terms for example, the prohibition of which had been an objective high on the list of positivist goals. To make matters worse, philosophers of science have more recently discovered that scientific terms change their meanings with the advent of new theories. Historians of science have documented these changes and have further pointed out that many scientific terms are metaphors, old terms that are given new meanings when they are used to suggest new hypotheses in new theories. That science utilizes metaphors is not accidental, for without them it would be impossible to pose a novel hypothesis intelligibly. The scientific need for metaphors undermined the belief that *all* scientific language was unambiguous, precise, and clear. Here was a species of a language that was both essential for the enterprise and also ambiguous, imprecise, and, at times, vague. Although many scientific terms may be precisely stipulated, in the scientific metaphor we find a usage that cannot be eliminated and for which we cannot specify a precise meaning.

Among philosophers of science, the issues of confirmation and meaning are still widely debated, but the discussion takes place in a context of awareness that the earlier hopes of positivists for a simple criterion of meaning based upon some principle of empirical testability are no longer tenable. Nor can one look at scientific language as if its meaning were fixed and precise. Nevertheless, most philosophers of religion have carried on the debate about the meaningfulness of religious language as if these developments in the philosophy of science had never taken place. Debates still rage about whether religious statements like "God exists" can be falsified in the belief that when such an utterance has been shown to be unfalsifiable, all of religious language has been eliminated as meaningless. Or, theologians defend religious language as having a meaning of its own in the belief that if the standards of meaning applicable to scientific language were applied to religious discourse, religious men would be exposed to the world as speakers of nonsense. The plain fact is that if the criteria of meaning that have been used to indict religious speech as meaningless were applied in the same way to scientific utterances, then scientific language would fall under the same indictment. In the first two chapters we shall explore in some detail both the development of this newer view of scientific language that acknowledges the need for metaphor, and the attempts to demonstrate the meaningfulness of religious lanaguage.

The discovery that the indictment of religious language is based upon faulty assumptions about scientific language does not, however, by itself render religious language meaningful. There could well be other reasons why religious discourse was composed of nonsense. To argue the contrary, we shall attempt to show that both scientists and theologians employ metaphors in the same meaningful manner. Our demonstration will consist of the development of a linguistic theory of metaphor, applicable to both scientific and religious usages, in which we describe how new meanings that are also intelligible can be suggested in metaphors. We will not argue that the contents of both scientific and religious metaphors are the same, nor that the intentions behind these metaphors are similar, but that the linguistic methods by which both enterprises achieve legitimate meanings are the same.

For the past fifteen years, literary critics and philosophers of language have shown a renewed interest in metaphor. During this period, what is now called the "tension theory of metaphor" has been developed. Consisting really in many, rather than one, interpretations of metaphor, all center in the notion that a metaphor can be best characterized by the "tension" or surprise that it causes in the hearer by means of its absurdity. When the two referents of a metaphor are read literally, they produce shock in the hearer either because of their oddity in expression or because they generate a contradiction. In the tension theory, metaphors suggest new meanings that may at first seem impossible to the hearer; but upon further consideration they partially express an experience or perception similar to his own. Without this analogy to his own experience, the person who confronts a new metaphor would find it unintelligible. Drawing upon this body of literature, we extend the tension theory by claiming that there are two aspects of metaphors, the suggestive and the expressive, each of which often becomes the prime characteristic of any particular metaphor. This distinction is crucial for the consideration of scientific and religious metaphors, for when critics argued that religion was meaningless because its metaphors were not reducible to ordinary language, they were only considering the suggestive metaphor and ignoring the expressive metaphors that abound not only in science, but in religion also. Critics denied meaning to religious discourse on the grounds that its metaphors were "irreducible." Against the irreducibility thesis, we argue not only that religious men utter expressive metaphors capable of confirmation in human experience, but that both forms of metaphor, suggestive and expressive, are meaningful linguistic devices.

We also extend the tension theory by considering metaphor to be a process rather than a static grammatical category. Some metaphors may begin linguistic life as startling suggestions, and then through confirmation in experience or experiment become more expressive than suggestive, and finally through continued use cease to be metaphors and become parts of ordinary language when they have lost their tension completely. Not all metaphors, however, traverse this path, for there are many, such as poetic metaphors or scientific hypotheses or theological terms that remain largely suggestive and never complete the cycle.

Just as there are different types of metaphors (some that primarily exemplify the suggestive aspect and others that exemplify the expressive aspect), so there are basically two different uses of metaphor. One is the normal use when we take a familiar word and employ it to suggest a new meaning; these metaphors convey suggestive meanings and ideas with more or less analogy to our own experience. These metaphors of conveyance, whether more suggestive or expressive, are the usual metaphors with which we are familiar as they are found in literature, religion, and science. There is, however, another use for metaphor, that of serving as the basic assumption underlying the way in which we describe the entire enterprise of science or religion. Called "root-metaphors," these hypothetical suggestions about the nature of the world offer possible ways of interpreting experience. The whole enterprise of science may be erected upon the metaphoric notion that "the world is mathematical" which is known to be literally false, and yet, we can construct theories upon the basis of treating the world "as if" it were mathematical. Similarly, "root-metaphors" like "God is wholly other" are hypothetical suggestions for formulating a theology rather than a literal description, for we know that if God were actually "*wholly* other" then we could have no knowledge of him. The use of these root-metaphors enables us to formulate hypothetical descriptions of the world and our experience. Ultimately, we do not understand the nature of things and so we speculate about them on the basis of hypotheses and categories derived from analogy to our everyday experience. Where these analogies prove to be fruitful, we pursue further. One of the decisive turning points in the history of science came in the seventeenth century when men sought to describe the physical world in mathematical terms that were then used to predict events that could be confirmed or disconfirmed in experiment or observation.

Along with the beneficial power of explanation that a root-metaphor offers comes the temptation to transform the root-metaphor into a myth by adopting that theory founded upon it as a literal description of how things are. By accepting a theoretical description as a literal one, men have over and over again transformed a speculative and hypothetical understanding into a myth. Those who became so convinced by the explanatory power of Newtonian mechanics that they came to believe that the world actually was composed of corpuscular particles located at spatio-temporal points, removed Newton's view of the physical world from the status of a tentative theory and transformed it into a myth. And only when Einstein's relativity theory offered an alternative to the Newtonian view did many scientists realize that they had wrongly claimed finality for the earlier theory. From the perspective of later theories it becomes easy to see that earlier theories are inadequate; yet the lesson that one ought not to attribute reality to these theories seems to come hard. Through familiarity with the theory and with the accumulation of large numbers of confirmations, researchers often come to believe that things really are the way that the theory suggests they are. By such assents, however, we forget the tentative nature of the theory and the hypothetical nature of the root-metaphor upon which it rests and create a myth.

Religious believers have for centuries created myths by taking speculative descriptions of reality and claiming that they were literal. Theologians spend much of their time trying to unlock these myths through interpretation. They seek the presuppositions behind the speculations hoping to recover the beliefs and feelings of those who offered the theological speculations. For some time, contemporary theologians have realized that myths were not "fictional stories" written by ignorant men. Rather, they were explanations of human experience based upon tentative hypotheses that became myths when men took them to be literal descriptions of the way things are. Biblical accounts of creation sought in primitive stories to express the belief that God had created the world. Although the writers may not have viewed the story as tentative, from our perspective there are numerous stories like the Genesis account that appear in various religious scriptures, and we know that such stories were based upon highly speculative theories. Similarly, many of the scientific theories formulated in the seventeenth, eighteenth, and nineteenth centuries were not thought of by the proposers as tentative, but contemporary scientists know, after having lived through several revolutions in scientific theory, that any theory is necessarily hypothetical and possibly may be superceded in the future by a different and more comprehensive theory. Myths are always discovered in retrospect when a later theory supplants an earlier one. But those who are aware that myths are created by attributing reality to theories erected upon speculative root-metaphors can avoid the creation of myths by such an awareness. Myths are to be avoided for they often inhibit the consideration of new hypotheses. By avoiding myths we do not wish to eliminate the contents of those myths, for their contents are the speculative hypotheses that may yield genuine insights into the nature of the empirical world or of human experience. What we want to avoid is the trap of committing oneself to a theoretical explanation as the absolute and final description of reality.

The notion of myth that we present in this work will be controversial, for many want to assert that myths are false stories about the gods or the creation of the world that have been superceded by scientific theories. They contrast the superstition of mythology with the rationality of science. Science with its formulation of theories based upon mathematics and its confirmation of predictions in experiments cannot, they believe, be like the wild speculative association of ideas that seems to be characteristic of mythology. Certainly there is no question that modern descriptions of the world are more rational than ancient ones in that contemporary theorists employ deductive and inductive procedures along with methodological tests in the empirical world. By contrast, traditional myths about the world associated ideas, but they often did seek confirmation in empirical events. Ritual ceremonies conducted to bring about fertility were judged by results and if no rain came, attention was given to the ceremony itself to see if it had been faulty. Occasionally, after repeated failure, a different ceremony based upon a different set of beliefs was employed. More often, when failure came and no imperfections could be found in the ceremony, it was continued in spite of these negative results. Such procedures are very similar to the response of modern scientists who, when confronted with unexpected negative results, first check their experimental apparatus and, if they find no faults, seldom abandon their theory unless another more comprehensive theory that can account for those negative results has already been proposed. Both the primitive man and the modern scientist create myths by believing that their explanation of the nature of the world is the absolute and final one. Myth results from the mistaken attribution of reality to a hypothetical description. Primitive man did not have the historical perspective to learn that most theories are replaced by other later theories and that to commit oneself to any theory as the proper and ultimate view of the nature of things also commits oneself to what is most likely later to be adjudged a myth. The explanations of modern man are more rational and better corroborated than those of ancient man, but the act by which both created myths was the same, that of infusing reality into a tentative and speculative hypothesis (a root-metaphor). Modern man, with his confidence that his explanations are so superior to primitive ones, faces the additional temptation of believing that since he is so much more rational, his theories cannot become myths. With this assumption and seduced by familiarity, scientists and theologians, knowing full well that their theories are built upon hypotheses, still often gradually fall into the trap of believing that they have discovered the way things really are. With our superior intelligence and rationality, how could the world and experience not be the way that our theories suggest?

Although we argue that scientists and theologians create myths in the same way by wrongly attributing reality and finality to hypothetical descriptions of the physical world and human experience, the contents of these myths are vastly different. We have already noted that the deductive and mathematical nature of scientific theories leads interpreters to argue that it is improper to label those theories, like the Newtonian view of the world that was once taken literally, as myths. Unquestionably, both the contents and the intention of scientific theory and theology are different; scientists seek to present explanations that describe the physical world while theologians attempt to describe various dimensions of human experience. Recognizing these differences, those comparing science and religion have often argued that scientific theories stress cognitive aspects of knowledge by employing mathematical laws and experimental test procedures while theological explanations stress emotive feelings by expressing the attitudes of individuals and groups towards the meaning and purpose of life. While it is certainly true that religion attends to values and feelings more than it does to the nature of the empirical world, the claim that religion expresses only emotive feelings and possesses no cognitive content is far too strong. Nor is science purely cognitive; the feelings and attitudes of scientists do affect the very character of scientific theories that are accepted or rejected. Theological explanations contain both factual statements and expressions of universal feelings that are not limited to subjective feelings. The descriptions of the world that science offers and the descriptions of human experience that theology offers do have major differences; theology, for instance, lacks the predictive aspects of science. And while theology exalts values as integral parts of its explanations, science seeks to minimize them. There are, however, also certain similarities in the two explanatory accounts. First, they both employ language in a similar fashion; there are not two languages, a language of religion and a language of science, but one language, ordinary discourse that is modified in like manner by both enterprises to form the metaphors of conveyance and root-metaphors. Scientific explanations do employ mathematics within the context of a conceptual theoretical framework. Too often observers of science have been so blinded by this mathematical usage that they have assumed that all scientific language was mathematical or at least representable in logical form. But much scientific language is necessarily not mathematical, for without speculative metaphors it would be difficult, if not impossible, to formulate new theories. Mathematics is embedded in scientific language rather than serving as the primary mode of linguistic expression with non-mathematical terms viewed as failures in precision and clarity. Observers of religion have been similarly blinded, not by clear and distinct mathematical expressions, but by the metaphoric and poetic aspects of religious language. This led critics to the hasty conclusion that religion had no cognitive or testable content. They forgot that theologians offer statements expressive of human experience as confirming doctrinal claims and that theology does include some factual and historical statements.

In spite of the differences between the two kinds of explanatory accounts, their different intentions, the use of mathematics and prediction by science, the emphasis upon feeling and value by religion, there are enough similarities in linguistic usage to suggest that they originate in a single conceptual approach to the nature of explanation. We can do no more than to speculate upon the character of this conceptual design for to do so more extensively would require a careful and thorough investigation into the nature of epistemology. Our speculations here will be based upon certain linguistic usages, metaphor and myth, of the scientific and theological enterprises. We shall suggest that both scientific theories and theologies can be understood as different forms of an abstract conceptual pattern of explanation in which the parts fit together to form a whole. Logic does not form the basis of the structure as the pattern is more like a visual picture in which there may be geometrical or proportional relationships among the parts, but these relationships are not primary, for what gives order and harmony to the picture is the sense of coherence that we have when we view it. Our familiarity with various patterns of explanation and our confidence that they do cohere enables us to accept such accounts as legitimate modes of understanding. Although it is very difficult to give an adequate and precise definition of the nature of a scientific theory, by acquaintance through experience every scientists can recognize one. In a like manner, a theologian can recognize a theological explanation when he sees one. What constitutes a legitimate conceptual pattern of explanation does change over a long period of time just as tastes in art change. Since the time of Euclid, the axiomatic system of deduction has been a candidate for the role of the best possible form of explanation. Yet historical explanations and scientific explanations that are not solely mathematical have challenged the supremacy of the deductive account as the best conceptual pattern. Our suggestions about a common conceptual pattern that underlies both the scientific and theological accounts of explanation must remain speculative since the evidence that we will examine from the language of science and the language of religion will be limited and in this study we shall not have sufficient time or space to develop a full-fledged theory of knowledge. That task remains for the future.

Most of our effort in this work will be devoted to establishing our thesis that science and religion use language in a similar manner; both employ metaphors to suggest new hypotheses, both seem to confirm their hypotheses in human experience, and both often create myths by forgetting the hypothetical character of their metaphors. In presenting this thesis, we shall have to pay close attention to recent developments in the philosophy of science and in the philosophy of religion. Issues in these areas will have to be developed with enough clarity and depth to support our thesis. Possible negative challenges will also have to be faced. In pursuing these debates, however, we shall have to resist the temptation to follow these issues to their conclusions. Many of these problems could occupy works far longer than this one, but to pursue them much further than we have would be to distract the reader from the main thesis.

Metaphor and myth in science and religion

I

The nature of scientific language

Philosophy of science arose as a discrete field of study in the twentieth century not only because philosophers wanted to generalize about the activities of scientists, but also because those philosophers who rode the crest of the rising tide of logical positivism were convinced that the language of science was the linguistic candidate most worthy of attention. Early positivists believed that language was meaningful if it was either tautologous or capable of empirical verification, and whereas logic and mathematics fulfilled the first part of this criterion of meaning, science preeminently fulfilled the latter.[1] Other languages, like that of traditional metaphysics or ethics or religion, were rejected as unworthy of attention because they were meaningless. Convinced that science was a storehouse of meaningful language, early positivists like Schlick, Neurath, Feigl, and Carnap focused their energy on the analysis of science. They investigated the nature of scientific explanation, the constitution of laws, and the procedures for confirmation. Behind all of this study lurked their presupposition that scientific language was meaningful and significant primarily because it was empirically verifiable. No matter how complicated and elaborate the theoretical construction, one could always confirm the theory (or disconfirm it) by publicly observable experiments. This was the bedrock of objectivity that distinguished scientific language from the language of morals or religion that could not be grounded in common observable experiences.

To protect scientists from the charge that theoretical terms were just as speculative and unverifiable as many metaphysical terms, positivists also endeavored to show that theoretical terms could be derived from obser-

1. A classic statement of logical positivism was given by A. J. Ayer in his *Language Truth and Logic* (New York: Dover Books, 1952) first published in 1935. In the preface to this second edition, Ayer weakens some of his claims but leaves the essential program intact.

vation terms. To sustain this defense, Rudolf Carnap proposed his famous program of using logical relations to reduce theoretical terms to observation terms. In doing so he revealed another presupposition held by positivists, that scientific terms were precise and rational in the sense that they could be expressed in logical propositions. By contrast, speculative metaphysical terms could not be "reduced" in the logical sense to observation terms.

As philosophy of science developed in the hands of positivists, an account of the nature of scientific explanation was offered by Hempel and Oppenheim that synthesized the notions that scientific language was precise, logical, and could be verified by observation.[2] This was the famous hypothetico-deductive or deductive-nomological account in which events are predicted by deduction from a combination of initial conditions and laws. Under this view, a distinction between theoretical and observation terms is presumed along with the belief that predicted events can be tested empirically.

From this perspective, philosophers subjected religious language to its most severe criticism. Religious language was anything but logical and precise and it could not be verified by an empirical test in the same way as scientific language under the hypothetico-deductive interpretation. Highly ambiguous, metaphorical, unverifiable directly, religious language not only could be labelled unscientific (a surprise to no one), but also would be indicted as meaningless at the court of positivist justice which associated meaning with verifiability.

To demonstrate that this indictment is faulty, we shall explore what has happened to the hypothetico-deductive account of scientific explanation and to the accompanying view of scientific language. Few philosophers of science today believe that scientific language is always precise or always directly verifiable or that all theoretical terms can be reduced to observation terms. There are two widely divergent sources for this change in view. The first arose within the tradition of positivism itself when objections were raised to the principle of verification, to reductionism, and to the logical structure of the hypothetico-deductive account of explanation.

2. Carl G. Hempel and Paul Oppenheim, "Studies in the Logic of Explanation," *Philosophy of Science*, 15 (1948), 135–175. We shall have much more to say about this shortly.

The second comes from historians of science and from philosophers of science who paid close attention to what scientists actually do. Both groups found the deductive account of explanation inadequate, citing numerous counterexamples and, most importantly, noting that scientists often constructed theories that not only replaced earlier ones but also changed the meanings of terms that had appeared in the earlier theory. How, then, could a new theory contain statements that falsified statements derived from the earlier theory when the terms found in those statements meant different things in each theory? This is the problem of meaning variance and it delivered a serious blow to the hypothetico-deductive account of positivists since, under their view, science was a cumulative affair where statements from earlier theories were falsified by statements implied by later theories. If a theory influences the meaning of a term, then the differentiation between theoretical and observation terms seems unnecessary, for all terms become theory-laden in the sense that there are no terms that are theory-neutral. Positivists had already found both that reductionism failed and that it was difficult, if not impossible, to give an adequate justification of the distinction between the two kinds of terms. Yet, they were unwilling to concede that there could be no distinction for to deny that would be to rob science of much of its objectivity. Without a language of observation that was independent of the theory under question, there would be no way to make tests that were objective. Theories might guarantee their own confirmation by determining in advance the nature of the substantive evidence. When confronted with alternative theories, a scientist would have to choose on the basis of personal or group preferences rather than on the basis of hard data. Thomas Kuhn's views presented in his *The Structure of Scientific Revolutions* are most often associated with the view deplored by many as leading directly to subjectivism.[3] His more recent disavowal notwithstanding, Kuhn does come close to looking at the choice of theories in sociological terms involving group practices and prejudices rather than in terms of objective tests.[4] The paradigms under which scientists inter-

3. Thomas S. Kuhn, *The Structure of Scientific Revolutions* (Chicago: University of Chicago Press, 1962).
4. See Kuhn's "Postscript—1969" to the second edition of *The Structure of Scientific Revolutions* (Chicago: University of Chicago Press, 1970).

pret the physical world include not only research practices derived from the adoption of a particular theory, but also personal commitments to certain values. The shift from one paradigm to another is described as a "conversion" of scientists. Even though Kuhn and others like Toulmin, Hanson, and Feyerabend have scored a major point against the positivistic view that stresses the deductive account of explanation by stressing meaning variance among theories, the victory is not without costs. We believe that the historical evidence in favor of meaning variance is overwhelming, but that to let it stand without some account of how objectivity in science is still possible would be almost to put scientific language on the same plane with religious language and, much as we wish to show the similarities between the two, we believe that such a move goes too far. Thus, we shall discuss not only the breakdown of the deductive account, but also the issues and problems raised by the newer view of science.

Our procedure in this chapter will be to review the positivist program for the deductive account of explanation, explore the objections to it, consider the rise of the view of science that emphasizes changes in both theories and meanings, and then to draw from these developments observations about the nature of scientific language. Our aim will be, as stated in the introduction, to show that the critique of religious language was based upon untenable assumptions about scientific language and to assess the similarities between the two forms of language. Much of that assessment cannot come until after a careful scrutiny of religious language, but in the present chapter we shall be seeking obvious similarities that are not the result of hasty generalizations. We shall maintain that both scientists and theologians necessarily employ metaphors, but the kinds that they use will be different. We shall maintain also that both scientific and religious terms are theory-laden, but we shall have to show just what that means and also suggest the limitations upon that notion for by itself it would suggest that science possesses no external objectivity.

The deductive account of explanation, as first formulated by Hempel and Oppenheim and still widely debated in that form, divides a scientific explanation into two parts: the explanans (that which explains) and the explanandum (that which is explained).[5] The explanans consists of a set of sentences $C_1, C_2, \ldots, C_k$ that establish the initial conditions and a set

5. Hempel and Oppenheim, "Studies in the Logic of Explanation."

of sentences $L_1, L_2, \ldots, L_r$ that represent general laws. From a combination of C's and L's an event in the empirical world, E, is deduced. The following diagram depicts the form of this account of explanation.

$$C_1, C_2, \ldots, C_k$$

Explanans

$$L_1, L_2, \ldots, L_r$$

$$\overline{E}$$ Explanandum

If event E has already occurred, then $C_1, C_2, \ldots, C_k$ and $L_1, L_2, \ldots, L_r$ can be called the explanation of that event. If E is deduced from the C's and L's, then E is a prediction and can be tested by observation.

Hempel and Oppenheim also lay down logical and empirical conditions of adequacy for this account. The former include the requirement that the explanandum must be a logical consequence of the explanans, the explanans must contain general laws, and the explanans must contain empirical content. The sole empirical condition of adequacy is that the sentences composing the explanans must be true. If these sentences were only highly confirmed, then it would be possible for further evidence to disconfirm them thereby making a logical deduction impossible.

There are numerous explanations in science that the deductive account actually does describe rather accurately. When one wants to compute the motion of a body at relatively slow speeds (compared to the speed of light), he begins with the initial position, velocity, and force impressed upon the body and applies the appropriate Newtonian law of motion expressed as a differential equation, and then deduces by computation the location and speed of the body at a later specified time. Or knowing the initial pressure and volume (under constant temperature), one can compute the new pressure of a gas in a new volume given by Boyle's law $P_1 V_1 = P_2 V_2$.

In considering the deductive account of explanation, how does one discover the general laws in the first place? If these are empirical generalizations derived from observation of data, then it might be possible that event E had already been confirmed and was the basis for the formulation of the law. To claim later that the general law was then the explanation for event E could be construed as circular reasoning. Consider as an example, Boyle's accidental discovery of the law that we know by his name.[6] He was not trying to investigate the relationship between pressure and volume, but began his experiment with the intention of demonstrating that air pressure was the sole cause of lifting a column of mercury 29.5 inches. Toricelli had earlier discovered this phenomenon and had aroused considerable discussion as to why the mercury rose in the tube. Some, like Boyle, claimed that the rise of mercury was caused by air pressure or as he called it, the "spring" of the air. Others, however, thought this highly implausible, for if air had pressure, then we should feel it on our bodies and we do not feel any such push or spring. Alternative hypotheses were constructed to explain the rise of the mercury. An invisible "funiculus" or membrane that pulled the mercury up a distance of only 29.5 inches was proposed by Franciscus Linus, and Boyle set out to devise an experiment that would refute him. Boyle knew that he could not merely repeat Toricelli's experiment with a column of mercury for Linus could still contend that it was the funiculus rather than the pressure of air that caused the mercury to go up. Instead, Boyle constructed a J-tube in which the longer side of the J was open to the air and the shorter one closed. Beginning with some mercury in the bottom of the tube, he then filled it with enough mercury so that the difference between the level of the shorter and longer sides was exactly 29.5 inches. This corresponded to the situation of a barometer with a tube set in a dish of mercury and was open to either interpretation, as caused by air pressure or by an invisible funiculus. Then Boyle added more mercury and the levels of mercury increased in both sides of the tube, but much more rapidly in the open side than in the closed one. To measure the difference in levels, Boyle put a scale on the closed side. The fact that mercury could rise further than 29.5 inches clearly refuted Linus's funiculus theory which had equated the strength of the invisible membrane (funiculus) as being only that which could lift 29.5 inches of mercury. Boyle varied the heights of mercury and noted the levels on both sides of the tube. The scale on the shorter side also measured the volume in the closed glass while the height on the open side measured the pressure. When these measurements were set down side by side, Boyle saw the inverse correlation between volume and pressure and proposed his famous law. He did not know about the need

6. "Robert Boyle's Experiments in Pneumatics," ed. James Bryant Conant, in *Harvard Case Histories in Experimental Science*, ed. James Bryant Conant (Cambridge: Harvard University Press, 1957).

for a constant temperature, but since the temperature of his laboratory seems to have varied only sightly, his results were not jeopardized.

From an event E, the proportionality between the heights of mercury in the two sides of the tube, Boyle was able to formulate his law, $P_1V_1 = P_2V_2$. The inference from the data, the lists of heights of mercury, to the law was clearly inductive as he moved from a number of instances to a universal law true for all cases. Now, to turn around and argue that Boyle's law as part of the explanans deductively predicted event E would seem to be circular since E had already been accepted as one of the premises in the formulation of the law itself.

Defenders of the deductive account of explanation were not particularly bothered by this charge of circularity, for they assumed an explicit distinction between the ways in which laws were discovered and the justification of a scientific explanation. Hans Reichenbach urged a distinction between the context of discovery and the context of justification.[7] The way in which a scientist discovered a law had no effect upon the validity of the law itself. He might dream of the solution or have a vision of a snake swallowing its own tail as Kekulé did in 1865 when he first conceived of the benzine ring, and that would in no way prejudice our decision to accept or reject the law or theory. Similarly, the fact that inductive inference from a series of events formed the basis for a law did not prevent one from using that same law to explain later events of the same kind that formed the data for the induction. This was possible because the explanatory account of an event was to be judged by its logical rigor and its confirmation or disconfirmation by the empirical event E.

Although the method of constructing a law did not worry deductivists, the nature of the law itself has proved to be bothersome. In his first formulation, Hempel attempted to express laws in the universal logical form: $(x)\ (A(x) \supset B(x))$.[8] He wanted to avoid calling sentences like "Every apple in basket b at time t is red" laws.[9] Those laws that are purely universal are called "fundamental laws" while those that are limited in scope and which can be derived from fundamental laws are

7. Hans Reichenbach, *Experience and Prediction* (Chicago: University of Chicago Press, 1961), pp. 5ff.
8. Hempel and Oppenheim, "Studies in the Logic of Explanation," pt. III.
9. Ibid., p. 153.

called "derivative laws." Hempel also strives to show that laws can be represented successfully in a lower functional calculus of logic, L. In such a logic, a "fundamental theory" corresponds to a "fundamental law." Hempel offered the following definitions of potential explanans and explanans.

An ordered couple of sentences, (T,C), constitutes a potential explanans for a singular sentence E if and only if the following conditions are satisfied:
  (1) T is essentially generalized and C is singular
  (2) E is derivable in L from T and C jointly
  (3) T is compatible with at least one class of basic sentences which has C but not E as a consequence.

An ordered couple of sentences, (T,C) constitutes an explanans for a singular sentence E if and only if
  (1) (T,C) is a potential explanans for E
  (2) T is a theory and C is true.[10]

Later under criticism of the above definitions, Hempel was forced to limit T to purely generalized sentences.[11]

In spite of the difficulties of defining a "law," the proponents of the deductive account of explanation had constructed an extremely useful instrument for the interpretation of scientific activity.[12] By means of it, science could be seen as a rational and objective activity. It was rational in the sense that the explanations offered by scientists could be described in logical terms like the definition of the explanans given above. And the empirical events, E, were predicted by deductive inference, that strongest form of rational assertion. It was objective in the sense that the events deduced from the explanans were capable of verification in the empirical world. Along with glories of rationality and objectivity, the deductive account also brought with it the bonuses of making sci-

10. Ibid. The first part of this definition appears as (7.8) on pp. 163–164 and the second as (7.6) on p. 160. Hempel offers them together. Cf. p. 164.

11. Ibid. Carl G. Hempel, "Postscript (1964) to Studies in the Logic of Explanation," in *Aspects of Scientific Explanation* (New York: The Free Press, 1965). This is one of those frustrating places forewarned in the introduction where we cannot pursue the threads of the debate for to do so would lengthen this work unduly.

12. The definition of "law" remains unsettled. Cf. Ernest Nagel, *The Structure of Science* (New York: Harcourt, Brace & World, 1961), ch. 4, and Peter Achinstein, *Law and Explanation* (Oxford: Oxford University Press, 1971), chs. 1–3.

ence a cumulative and progressive enterprise and of offering a dividing line between science and metaphysics. Under the deductive interpretation of explanation, a scientist can test the validity of a theory by resorting to observation or experiment. Since the explanation itself is of a logical form, if the experiment fails, then by modus tollens, the theoretical hypothesis will be falsified.[13] If the experiment succeeds repeatedly, then the theory will be corroborated. By means of confirmation of various events, E, theories will be confirmed and added to the accumulation of scientific information already available. Science will progress through the continued accumulation of confirmed theories. Those disconfirmed will be discarded and our confidence in the progress of science will be supported by our logical procedures and empirical tests. These twin stalwarts of logic and empiricism are also those factors which served to differentiate science from metaphysics. Speculative philosophers could rarely set their metaphysical accounts of the world in a logical framework that was empirically testable. If the metaphysician claimed that a term like "substance" was meaningful because it could be generalized from perception, the positivist philosopher of science could object that such a generalization could not be expressed in logic and that such terms were superfluous and ought to be eliminated. When the metaphysician turned the tables and charged that scientists also employed theoretical terms like "force" or "mass" that were not directly observable, the positivist would reply that theoretical terms could be reduced to observation terms (reductionism) or, during the heyday of the deductive account, that rules of correspondence (partial interpretations) were available to relate the two types of terms.[14] Along with the deductive-nomological account of explanation, philosophers of science presumed both that a careful distinction between observation and theoretical terms could be made and, further, that there existed a legitimate procedure by which the meanings of theoretical terms could be derived from observation terms. Scientific terms of both the observational and theoretical variety were also assumed to be precise since, if they were not, then the logical deduction from the explanans to the explanandum would fail. Strict logical deduction requires that equivocal

---

13. A more detailed account of falsifiability and explanation will follow shortly.
14. I intend to deal with this problem more extensively later.

meanings and ambiguity be removed. Accordingly, these philosophers of science sought to define their terms as carefully as possible and to insure that, whenever possible, theoretical terms be specified by stipulated logical relations to well defined observation terms. "Logic" and "testability" became the highest values for the positivist philosophers of science.

From the pinnacle of success, some positivist philosophers turned their glance towards religious language. In contrast to scientific language, it was imprecise, ambiguous, and incapable of empirical test. The unobservable terms of religion could not be related to observable experience by means of logical relationships. Demands were made that if religious language is to be considered meaningful, it must be capable of verification in the same manner as scientific language. Debates raged over whether religious utterances were in fact capable of verification. Clever proposals that religious discourse could be verified after death and, therefore, were technically "verifiable" and thereby meaningful, were put forth by apologists. Other theologians retreated into the security of mysticism or religious experience believing that science and religion existed in two entirely different realms of human experience.

By the rational standards of the deductive account of science, the mythical explanations offered by religion seemed irrational. Even those existential interpretations of human experience based upon a demythologization of traditional stories seemed irrational and subjective. How could such interpretations and commitments be tested in public? No objectivity could be possible when the faithful projected their religious symbols onto human experience. Different religions owned different symbols and universal agreement about them seemed impossible.

If science really was as the deductivists claimed, then, perhaps, their criticisms of religious language could be construed as legitimate and fair. But, just as the deductive account achieved success and notoriety, severe problems within it were discovered that seriously undermined the beliefs about the nature of scientific language by which religious language had been faulted. And it is to this account that we must now turn.

Positivists were convinced that the meaning of a sentence was identical with the way in which the truth or falsehood of that sentence was determined. And if there was no possible way to make that determination, then the sentence could be discarded as meaningless. Sentences that were tautologous were true by definition and were called analytic. Sentences not true by definition, synthetic sentences, could only be meaningful if they could be confirmed empirically. The empirical test most often proposed to serve as the basis for confirmation was observation of objects. Within the realm of science, although one could find numerous sentences that were testable by observation, one could also find synthetic sentences that contained nonobservable or theoretical terms that prevented confirmation by observation. To save science from the charge that it, like metaphysics, was partially untestable, positivist philosophers of science sought to demonstrate how theoretical terms could be logically reduced to observable terms.

Rudolf Carnap offered the most famous program of reduction in his paper, "Testability and Meaning."[15] Aware of the inadequacies of the principle of verification, he offered, instead, the notion of confirmation, acknowledging that complete confirmation is usually impossible since the field of observations is usually infinite. Confirmation was defined as the reduction of a sentence to a class of observable predicates. The major logical relation that Carnap used was the bilateral reduction sentence, $(Q_1 \supset Q_3 \equiv Q_2)$ in which Q_1 and Q_2 are properties composed of observable predicates $P_1, P_2, \ldots, P_n$. Q_3 may be a nonobservable theoretical term. Carnap also required that $(x)(-Q_1(x))$ not be valid for if it were, then the bilateral reduction sentence would always be true regardless of the values of Q_2 and Q_3, since a false antecedent always renders a true implication. Testable sentences were those sentences with observable predicates. Thus, all testable sentences were confirmable, but not all confirmable sentences were testable since confirmable sentences could be generated by the bilateral reduction sentence in which the nonobservable predicate Q_3 was related to Q_1 and Q_2 which were confirmed by sets of observable predicates. By defining meaning in terms of confirmability and by showing how to relate theoretical terms to predicates that were observable, Carnap offered a demarcation line between meaningful science and meaningless metaphysics.

Unhappily for positivists, the reduction program failed for there were

15. Rudolf Carnap, "Testability and Meaning," *Philosophy of Science*, 3, no. 4 (Oct., 1936), 420–471, and 4, no. 1 (Jan., 1937), 2–40.

too many theoretical constructions that could not be reduced via the bilateral reduction sentence to sets of observable predicates. And there was a basic dilemma formulated by Hempel at the very heart of the reductionist program which stated that if theoretical terms could be reduced, then they were unnecessary, and if they could not be reduced, then they did not serve their purpose and again were unnecessary.[16] Carnap himself came to recognize the weakness of his own program and proposed to replace it through introducing theoretical terms into science by means of partial interpretations.[17] These are the measurement techniques used by scientists as tests in their experiments and are also known as rules of correspondence. An investigator uses a theory to predict a certain event, E, and then constructs an experimental method of confirming or disconfirming that event. The construction of this test procedure consists in the formulation of rules of correspondence that relate theoretical terms like "mass" to empirically observable measurements. Instead of employing logical reduction, the positivists now sought to give empirical significance to scientific language by means of these partial interpretations.

But were partial interpretations sufficiently strong to distinguish the language of science with its unobservable theoretical terms from the language of metaphysics with its unobservable speculative terms? Achinstein answers no by presenting the following argument: if T is any postulate with M theoretical terms in it and O an observation statement, then a correspondence rule can be written as $O \supset T$.[18] We can, however, also construct the tautology, $T \supset (O \supset T)$ which means that any postulate, whether scientific or not can imply a correspondence rule. Israel Scheffler also modified the stringent claims of empiricists by admitting

16. Carl G. Hempel, "The Theoretician's Dilemma," *Minnesota Studies in the Philosophy of Science*, vol. 2, ed. Herbert Feigl, Michael Sciven and Grover Maxwell (Minneapolis: University of Minnesota Press, 1958). Hempel rejects the dilemma on the grounds that theoretical terms are desirable and that reduction is not possible.

17. Rudolf Carnap, "The Methodological Character of Theoretical Terms," *Minnesota Studies in the Philosophy of Science*, vol. 1, ed. Herbert Feigl and Michael Scriven (Minneapolis: University of Minnesota Press, 1956). Carnap also believes that dispositional terms can be introduced into the observation language but stresses partial interpretations as the more important way of introducing theoretical terms.

18. Peter Achinstein, "Theoretical Terms and Partial Interpretation," *The British Journal for the Philosophy of Science*, 14, no. 54 (Aug., 1962). Cf. also his "Rudolf Carnap, II," *The Review of Metaphysics*, no. 4 (June, 1966).

that many scientific statements are not translatable into an empirical language and that the absence of this reduction should not classify them as meaningless.[19] He argued that the translation of sentences into an empirical language is a sufficient, but not a necessary condition for empirical meaningfulness, and he claimed that those sentences which cannot be so mapped have an independent criterion of meaning. Metaphysicians and theologians have independent criteria of meaning and they formulate nonobservable terms that can produce the kind of tautologous statement suggested by Achinstein in which a rule of correspondence is embedded. By itself, the partial interpretation fails as a criterion of demarcation between science and metaphysics.

And from still another perspective, the reductionist program was attacked. In his famous paper, "Two Dogmas of Empiricism," Quine argued that the distinction between analytic and synthetic could not be made and reductionism, therefore, would also fail.[20] His arguments against the distinction were that either the notion of analytic is itself prior or it rests upon some form of extensional synonymy. This means that the user must presuppose the notion; an unacceptable procedure since it requires an a priori assumption contrary to the positivist's commitment to empiricism. Synonymy rests upon dictionary definitions which are extensional. Cognitive synonymy depends upon prior definitions of analytic, again unacceptable to an empiricist. Thus, Quine concluded that it is not possible to make the distinction. He thought that the failure of the distinction "blurred" the line between metaphysics and science.

Even before the proposals for a new interpretation of science by Kuhn and others, the distinction between observation and theoretical terms and the attempt to define the latter in terms of the former had been undermined by philosophical criticism. This failure did not guarantee the meaningfulness of metaphysics or theology. What it did was to eliminate

19. Israel Scheffler, "Theoretical Terms and a Modest Empiricism," in *Philosophy of Science*, ed. Arthur Danto and Sidney Morgenbesser, (New York: Meridian Books, 1960).

20. Willard Van Orman Quine, "Two Dogmas of Empiricism," in *From a Logical Point of View* (New York: Harper Torchbooks, 1961). For debates cf. also: Hilary Putnam, "The Analytic and the Synthetic," in *Minnesota Studies in the Philosophy of Science*, vol. 3, ed. Herbert Feigl and Grover Maxwell (Minneapolis: University of Minnesota Press, 1962); and H. P. Grice and P. F. Strawson, "In Defense of a Dogma," *Philosophical Review*, 65 (1956), 141ff.

the use of reductionism as a criterion of difference between science and nonscience. The failure also prevented positivists from claiming that metaphysics was meaningless solely because it employed nonobservable terms.

Advocates of the deductive account of explanation also encountered the problem of how to give empirical confirmation to events predicted by theories. The issue seems simple enough for one should merely observe the event predicted in order to confirm it. But how many confirmations must we have before we are certain that a particular event is confirmed? If there are an infinite number of possible confirmations, as there are in many empirical test situations, then complete certainty will never be possible.

Early positivists who wanted to use verification as their method of confirmation found that verification itself was subject to logical criticism. As Karl Popper showed in his classic, *The Logic of Scientific Discovery*,[21] in universal statements of the form $(x)(A (x) \supset B(x))$ even if $B(x)$ is fully confirmed (verified), $A(x)$ may be either true or false. Affirming the consequent of an implication does not insure the truth of the antecedent. Popper replaced the principle of verification by a principle of falsification. By denying the consequent $B(x)$, one is certain by modus tollens that the antecedent, $A(x)$, is also false. Popper believed that science proceeded by formulating conjectural hypotheses, and then tested them to find falsifications of them.[22] Hypotheses for which confirmations are found rather than falsifications will be held to be tentatively acceptable; we hold them as valid just until refutation appears. The more tests that we can apply to an hypothesis, the more falsifiable it is, and the more falsifiable, the more empirical. Falsifiability was also used by Popper as a principle of demarcation between science and metaphysics. He did not claim that

21. Karl R. Popper, *The Logic of Scientific Discovery* (New York: Science Editions, 1961).
22. Cf. also Karl R. Popper, "Science: Conjectures and Refutations," in his *Conjectures and Refutations: The Growth of Scientific Knowledge* (New York: Harper Torchbooks, 1968); Imre Lakatos has written an interesting account of the development of Popper's notion of falsifiability in his: "Criticism and the Methodology of Scientific Research Programmes," in *Proceedings of the Aristotelian Society*, 69, (1968–1969) pp. 149–186.

metaphysics was meaningless, but that it was different from science because it was not capable of falsification.[23]

When one applies the principle of falsifiability to the hypothetico-deductive account of scientific explanation, in a refutation, event E, the consequent is falsified and the antecedent is also rendered false. But what is that antecedent? Composed of a conjunction of applicable laws, $L_1, L_2, \ldots, L_r$, and initial conditions, $C_1, C_2, \ldots, C_k$, any one or any combination of the parts of that conjunction may be false. How do we identify which part of the conjunction, L_1 & L_2 & C_1 & C_2, makes the entire statement false? Is it L_1 alone, or L_1 and L_2, or C_1, or L_1 and C_1? The denial that the falsification of an event can falsify a single hypothesis has come to be known as the Duhem-Quine thesis as Duhem first articulated a similar view early in the twentieth century in his *The Aim and Structure of Physical Theory* and Quine more recently has reinforced this suggestion.[24] The literature on the Duhem-Quine thesis is a vast debate on whether there are counterexamples to the thesis and what are the consequences of it.[25] If one accepts the major thrust of the thesis that it is difficult to falsify a theory, as we do, then the invention of auxiliary hypotheses by scientists becomes one of the major implications of such a thesis. Many theories and laws are retained in the face of negative empirical evidence. Even after locating which part of the conjunction in the hypothesis is false, often one can still alter the conjunction with an auxiliary hypothesis to eliminate the difficulty. This also makes the

23. Karl R. Popper, "The Demarcation between Science and Metaphysics," in *Conjectures and Refutations*.

24. Pierre Duhem, *The Aim and Structure of Physical Theory* (Princeton: Princeton University Press, 1954); Williard Van Orman Quine, "Two Dogmas of Empiricism," in his *From a Logical Point of View* (New York: Harper Torchbook, 1963).

25. Adolf Grunbaum, "The Falsifiability of Theories: Total or Partial? A Contemporary Evolution of the Duhem-Quine Thesis," *Synthese*, 14, no. 1 (March, 1962), 17–34; Adolf Grunbaum, "Geometry, Chronometry, and Empiricism," *Minnesota Studies in the Philosophy of Science*, Vol. 3; Adolf Grunbaum, "The Falsifiability of a Component of a Theoretical System," *Mind, Matter, and Method*, ed. Paul K. Feyerabend and Grover Maxwell (Minneapolis: University of Minnesota Press, 1966); J. W. Swanson, "Discussion on the D-Thesis," *Philosophy of Science*, 34, no. 1 (March, 1967), 59–68; Gary Wedeking, "Duhem, Quine and Grunbaum on Falsification," *Philosophy of Science*, 36, no. 4 (Dec., 1969), 375–380; Philip L. Quinn, "The Status of the D-Thesis," *Philosophy of Science*, 36, no. 4 (Dec., 1969), 381–399; Jarrett Leplin, "Contextual Falsification and Scientific Methodology," *Philosophy of Science*, 39, no. 4 (Dec., 1972), 476–490.

comparison of theories extremely difficult, for if a crucial experiment seems to confirm one theory and falsify another, then it may be possible to patch up the faults of the one such that it no longer can be refuted. Or, it may not be possible even to specify a crucial experiment since one cannot locate the exact parts of the conjunctive hypothesis in each theory that are to be compared (one confirmed and the other falsified in the respective theories).

In spite of the difficulties of locating precisely what has been falsified in a theory, the principle of falsification did have a profound effect upon positivists. Both Carnap and Hempel, leading exponents of the deductivist view, abandoned verifiability in favor of falsifiability as the more conclusive empirical test.[26] Yet they still retained the notion that theories could be confirmed by empirical evidence. While they admitted that a theory could never be fully verified, it could be corroborated by a high degree of observable confirmation. A theory could be considered to be true if there was little or no negative evidence against it and there also existed a large amount of confirmatory evidence. If a conclusive negative instance were found, then the hypothesis ought to be replaced by another (assuming that it is identifiable in light of the Duhem-Quine thesis). For example, for a long time the statement, "All swans are white" was accepted as true since a large number of observations had been accumulated to lend this hypothesis a high degree of confirmation. When, however, black swans were discovered in Australia, the hypothesis was refuted.

The method of confirmation, however, also turned out to be fraught with problems. In an examination of the nature of confirmation, Hempel found that by the logical equivalence of S_1: $(x)(Raven(x) \supset Black(x))$ and S_2: $(x)(-Black(x) \supset -Raven(x))$, an object that was not a Raven and Black would confirm S_1. This discovery he called the "paradox of confirmation."[27] To eliminate this paradox and to clarify the concept of confirmation, Hempel proceeded to present a series of criteria that have

26. Rudolf Carnap, "Autobiography," in *The Philosophy of Rudolf Carnap*, ed. Paul A. Schilpp, (Evanston, Ill.: Library of Living Philosophers, 1964); Carl G. Hempel, *Philosophy of Natural Science* (Englewood Cliffs: Prentice-Hall, 1966).
27. Carl G. Hempel, "Studies in the Logic of Confirmation," reprinted in *Aspects of Scientific Explanation*.

been widely debated as to their success.[28] Into this discussion we cannot proceed further, but acknowledging the problem will serve to make us aware of just how difficult both falsification and confirmation can be in science. Hempel's paradox arises from construing scientific laws in terms of universal conditional statements. Even if we were to eliminate the requirement that laws be stated in terms of universals we would still be faced with the difficulty of determining when an even, E, had been confirmed (the problem of induction) and of how we locate what we have falsified when E turns out to be negative.

Thus far, we have seen that the hypothetico-deductive account of explanation met with serious difficulties both in trying to maintain a definite distinction between theoretical and observation statements, and in offering an adequate account of confirmation. Although these problems may shake our confidence in the deductive account, they may not be sufficiently damaging to warrant outright rejection. Every explanatory theory, whether deductive or inductive, may have problems in justifying its method of confirmation. And the difficulty of separating observation from theoretical terms may pose a threat to any account of scientific explanation. Some philosophers of science, however, found objections to the very nature of the hypothetico-deductive account of explanation.[29]

The first major objection was that the deductive account did not fit most of the theories used by scientists. By describing laws as universal conditionals, positivists had limited the scope of the deductive account severely. Even Newtonian laws when formulated as second order differential equations could not be construed as universal logical implications. When the equations of relativity or quantum mechanics were considered, the extreme simplicity of the universal conditional was exposed by con-

28. I. J. Good, "The Paradox of Confirmation," pts. I and II, *The British Journal for the Philosophy of Science,* 11 (1960), 145–148; 12 (1961), 63–64; J. L. Mackie, "The Paradoxes of Confirmation," *The British Journal for the Philosophy of Science,* 13 (1963), 256–277; B. A. Brody, "Confirmation and Explanation," *Journal of Philosophy,* 65, no. 10 (May 16, 1968) 282–299; J. W. N. Watkins, "The 'Paradoxes of Confirmation,'" in *The Critical Approach to Science and Philosophy,* ed. M. Bunge (New York: Free Press, 1964).
29. The literature on this problem is enormous. One of the most important early critiques was: Michael Scriven, "Explanations, Prediction, and Laws," *Minnesota Studies in the Philosophy of Science,* vol. 3. A more recent summary of many objections is found in ch. 5 of Achinstein's *Laws and Explanations.*

trast even more starkly. Scientific laws were much more complicated mathematically than positivists had allowed in their formulation of the deductive description of explanation. Hempel became aware of this limitation and modified his proposal to allow for probabilistic laws.[30] The same format is used for the description of probabilistic explanation as that employed for deductive explanation. There are initial conditions and laws, but the laws $L_1, L_2, . . ., L_r$ become laws expressed in probabilities rather than expressed in universal generalizations. Event E is no longer predicted by deduction from a conjunction of laws and initial conditions, but is predicted with a certain degree of probability. What was prediction by deductive inference has become prediction by inductive generalization on the basis of a certain probability. Hempel presents the example of exposure to measles with the resulting contraction of the disease. The law is: that it is highly probable that anyone exposed to measles will catch them, and the initial condition C is: that Jim was exposed to measles. The event E is: that Jim catches the measles, and this inference can be made on the inductive probability that it is highly probable that Jim will catch the measles. What has happened to the *deductive* nature of explanation in this shift? It has been eliminated altogether, and only the schema from the original deductive-nomological account remains, with L's, C's, and an E. Laws are no longer universal generalizations expressed in conditional form, rationality can be expressed in probability rather than as a form of modus ponens or modus tollens, and confirmation takes place by the enumeration of the frequency of confirmed instances.

Another problem with the deductive account was its ignorance of the context in which the explanation was offered. Hempel's formulation of another account of probabilistic explanation was, in part, a recognition that different kinds of explanations demand different descriptions of them. What constitutes an explanation in physics often differs from explanatory theories presented by biologists. Much of the early activity of positivists who advocated a hypothetico-deductive account was spent in attempting to show that teleological explanations of biology could be reduced to physical explanations and that terms like "purpose" and

30. Carl G. Hempel, "Deductive-Nomological vs. Statistical Explanation," *Minnesota Studies in the Philosophy of Science*, vol. 3, and his *Philosophy of Natural Science*.

"emergence" were unnecessary. Even within physics, however, explanations will vary. The kind of explanation offered by a researcher engaged in microwave spectroscopy differs in nature from that assumed by a physicist computing the inertial forces involved in sending rockets to the moon and nearby planets. Often the "depth" of an investigation determines the kind of explanation that can be considered satisfactory. The microwave spectroscopist deals with a set of laws applicable to molecular structure and radiation while the physicist treating inertial forces uses laws applicable to visible objects and their motion. To be sure, large visible objects are composed of molecules and even smaller particles, but there the laws describing these two levels of understanding are not reducible and often are not even compatible.

Attacks have also been made upon the identification of prediction with deduction. Before Hempel had formulated the probabilistic account, diagnostic examples from medicine were offered along with the citation of Darwin's evolutionary theory as explanatory accounts that offered predictions not based upon deduction.[31] It has also been shown that descriptions of events can be given in lawlike form with initial conditions that fit the deductive paradigm, but which few would concede are an adequate explanatory account. Achinstein claims that the diagnostic skill of a physician can be stated as a law: whenever a skilled physician declares that a patient under examination will die shortly, the patient will die shortly.[32] An initial condition would be the examination of the patient and the skilled physician's declaration that he will die shortly. The prediction is that the patient will die. Yet no one would claim that the doctor's diagnosis was the cause of the patient's death.

Before the advent of the newer view of science described by Toulmin, Hanson, Kuhn, and others which stresses the historical activity of scientists rather than the logic of explanation, the hypothetico-deductive account was in serious trouble. Having grown up in the positivist's beliefs that logic combined with empiricism would serve to justify the meaningfulness of any philosophical enterprise, the deductive account suffered from being too restricted in its scope of applicability. Far too few scientific

31. Cf. Michael Scriven, "Explanation and Prediction in Evolutionary Theory," *Science*, 130 (1959), 477–482.
32. Achinstein, *Law and Explanation*, p. 101.

laws can be represented as hypothetical universal statements and induction plays as large a role, or an even larger one, than does deduction in both explanation and prediction. The widespread debate, however, about the adequacy of the deductive-nomological description of explanation proved to be extremely fruitful for the philosophy of science as it identified not only the major issue of what constitutes an explanation, but also uncovered the sticky problems of confirmation and the relationship between observation and theory. These issues are not confined to discussion about positivistic interpretations of science, for, as we shall see shortly, they persist in alternative formulations of the nature of explanation.

During the last decade, an alternate view of science and of scientific explanation has been described by a number of philosophers and historians of science including Toulmin, Hanson, and Kuhn.[33] These writers stress the changes in scientific theories that one finds in reading the history of science rather than the logic of explanation that the defenders of the deductive account emphasized. The picture of scientific explanation that these new writers present is far less definite than that of the positivists since the distinction between discovery and justification is rejected and human attitudes and prejudices are introduced. Blurring the line between theoretical and observation terms makes the comparison of theories on a logical basis difficult. If scientific terms are dependent upon the theory in which they occur for their meaning, then, when the same term appears in two different theories, it will have different meanings in each theory. How can one then falsify a statement derived from a theory when the terms in that theory mean something different from what they mean in the new statement that is said to falsify the earlier one?

Although this "new" view of the philosophy of science pays more attention to the actual activities of scientists, it does bring with it a number of severe philosophical problems that the older view, the deductive account, did not possess. In the deductive nomological account, it was clear that reason consisted of the deductive inference and objectivity consisted in the testability of the events deduced (predicted or postdicted) by the conjunction of laws and initial conditions. We do not know so

33. Stephen Toulmin, *Foresight and Understanding* (New York: Harper Torchbooks, 1963); Norwood Russell Hanson, *Patterns of Discovery* (Cambridge: Cambridge University Press, 1958); Thomas S. Kuhn, *The Structure of Scientific Revolutions*.

precisely what reason signifies in the newer view; nor can we give as clear a definition of objectivity. To assess the nature of scientific language under this newer view of science, we shall first describe Thomas Kuhn's interpretation and then consider some of the criticism that has been levelled at his account.[34]

Kuhn begins his description of science by distinguishing between two kinds of science, normal science and revolutionary science.[35] The major activity of scientists engaged in normal science is that of puzzle-solving. Trained in graduate schools with standard textbooks by researchers who held an accepted theory, and having performed standard experiments themselves, young investigators seek to ply their trade by solving some of the unsolved puzzles of theory. The questions that they ask and the ways in which they conceive of experiments that will possibly answer those questions are largely determined by the theory which they hold and by the procedures that they consider to be proper for science. When they discover experimental results that answer their questions, journals manned by editors who hold the same beliefs are eager to publish their findings for such puzzle-solving adds to the storehouse of scientific knowledge. In this sense, normal science is cumulative and the account that Kuhn gives of it is like that given of the deductive accout by Hempel. Known laws are used to predict events that are then tested by experiment. Kuhn, however, differs from Hempel not only in not claiming that explanation under normal scientific activity must be subsumed under universals and deductions, but also in that disconfirmations of experiments are not claimed to refute theories. Under Kuhn's description, when the investigator seeking a solution to a puzzle receives a negative result, he sets aside the disconfirmation as an anomaly. Few scientists abandon theories when negative evidence appears. Either they demonstrate that such evidence results from experimental error or, if they cannot do that, then they set aside the negative information as unexplained. Most theories are held in spite of the existence of negative empirical evidence.

If a philosopher of science or an historian of science studies normal

34. We are using Kuhn's account since it is the most widely discussed of the three. Note that there are major differences among the three as Hanson stresses conceptual patterns in the Gestalt tradition and Toulmin wants to emphasize the evolutionary nature of concepts.

35. We shall use the second edition of Kuhn's *The Structure of Scientific Revolutions*, published in 1970, as the basis of our exposition.

science he will find that the common beliefs, accepted scientific procedures, values, and commonly held theories constitute a "paradigm." A
paradigm cannot be described by a set of rules, but can be better understood as a set of common commitments that scientists possess when they
are pursuing normal science.

Revolutionary science occurs when a paradigm-shift takes place.
Abandoning one paradigm is always accompanied by the simultaneous
acceptance of another paradigm. Newtonian mechanics were not abandoned until relativity theory was accepted. Before a paradigm-shift occurs, there is a crisis among believers in the old paradigm. Anomalies
accumulate in the old paradigm, auxiliary hypotheses are constructed to
meet these growing difficulties, and confidence in the ability of the
paradigm to solve traditional problems weakens. Kuhn cites the failure of
the Ptolemaic paradigm before Copernicus and the fragmentation of the
phlogiston theory into a myriad of versions before Lavoisier as examples
of the crises in paradigms that precede a paradigm-shift. In a crisis
situation, the lines of a paradigm are blurred and the normal procedures
for scientific investigation become less rigidly defined. Alternatives to the
reigning theory are proposed. Finally, a new paradigm emerges that gives
an alternate explanation and different experimental procedures. The new
paradigm may be radically different, like Einstein's relativity theory that
was based upon presuppositions completely different from Newtonian
mechanics. The absolute character of length and time were transformed
into quantities relative to the speed of light.

When a new paradigm appears, although its proponents strongly
believe that it can better interpret the phenomena under investigation,
acceptance by the scientific community may not follow immediately. The
early formulators of the new paradigm may even find it initially difficult
to publish their views, since journal editors and referees still hold firmly to
the old paradigm. Gradually, however, either through the circulation of
their views privately or by founding new journals to publish the new
view, the alternate paradigm becomes debated. Scientists consider it in
contrast with the old paradigm and also in light of its interpretation of
nature. If convinced, an individual scientist will discard the old paradigm
simultaneously adopting the new one. Kuhn describes this change as a
"conversion" and as a Gestalt shift, and claims that to abandon one

paradigm without at the same time adopting another one would be to abandon science itself. He also observes that some scientists, steeped in the traditional paradigm, never accept the new paradigm. And Kuhn quotes Max Planck that "a new scientific truth does not triumph by convincing its opponents and making them see the light, but rather because its opponents eventually die, and a new generation grows up that is familiar with it."[36]

The history of science reveals over and over again that new paradigms are accepted and displace older ones. When this happens, textbooks are rewritten, laboratory procedures changed, and the questions that investigators now ask are different. The acceptance of a new paradigm brings with it a return to normal science. Solving the puzzles generated by the new paradigm rather than worrying about which paradigm to accept becomes the major preoccupation of scientists. This completes the cycle from paradigm to crisis to revolution to accepted paradigm.

The chief criticism that Kuhn and others make of Hempel and the defenders of the deductive-nomological account of explanation is that their description of science fails to acknowledge the radical shift in the nature and structure of theories that can be found in the history of science. Science does not just accumulate data and acquire new theories by the logical process of contradiction with a later theory contradicting an earlier one. Instead, there are abrupt changes in the very meaning of theories such that contradiction is impossible when comparing two theories. Kuhn describes competing paradigms, and thereby the theories found within those paradigms, as incommensurable. They cannot be tested by crucial experiments because the terms of each theory are dependent upon that theory for their meaning. To claim that one theory generates statements that falsify similar statements generated by the other theory would be to equivocate upon the meaning of the terms appearing in seemingly contradictory statements. Kuhn claims that the process of writing textbooks in which anomalies and many other features of the crisis that precedes a revolution are eliminated accounts for the belief among many scientists that science moves ahead in a linear, cumulative fashion.

36. Max Planck, *Scientific Autobiography and Other Papers* (New York: 1949), pp. 33–34, as cited by Kuhn, p. 151.

Another primary difference resulting from the Kuhnian view as contrasted with the deductive account arises from Kuhn's contention that no observations can be made independent of theory. He claims that where Lavoisier had seen oxygen, Priestly had observed de-phlogisticated air. Looking at data is like wearing goggles that make us see in a particular way and the reigning theory accounts for the kind of glasses that we wear. Kuhn rejects a neutral language of observations as a "hopeless" defense of the objectivity of sensory experience.[37] If Kuhn is correct, then Hempel's objective confirmation of event E by empirical observation becomes doomed. By making observations dependent upon theory, circularity enters Hempel's program since the explanans will already contain within itself the explanandum and the deduction of E will be an illegitimate form of circular reasoning.

Objections to this newer interpretation of science were not slow in coming.[38] Along with objections to his historical examples, and criticism that he had used the notion of paradigm in a multitude of ways, the foremost charge was that Kuhn had robbed science of both its rationality and its objectivity and had turned it into an enterprise in which theories were accepted on the basis of social and political prejudices.[39] Israel Scheffler charges that Kuhn has refuted himself by first arguing that paradigm-shifts do not occur "by deliberation and interpretation" and then by appealing to evidence from the history of science to support his own new paradigm for the nature of explanation.[40] Paradigms determine the way in which the scientist looks at the world and there can be no logical contact between competing paradigms, according to Kuhn. Scheffler suggests that we consider the proposal of Kuhn for a new view of science as a paradigm-shift from the older view of Hempel (deductive-nomological). Parallels certainly do exist between the paradigm-shifts in science that Kuhn described and movements in the philosophy of science.

37. Kuhn, p. 126.

38. Among the many replies to Kuhn, two of the important books dealing with his work are: Israel Scheffler, *Science and Subjectivity* (Indianapolis: Bobbs-Merrill, 1967) and Imre Lakatos and Alan Musgrave, *Criticism and the Growth of Knowledge* (Cambridge: Cambridge University Press, 1970).

39. Cf. Margaret Masterman, "The Nature of a Paradigm," in *Criticism and the Growth of Knowledge.*

40. *Science and Subjectivity*, pp. 21–22, 53, 74. Cf. also Scheffler's "Vision and Revolution: A Postscript on Kuhn," *Philosophy of Science*, 39, no. 3 (Sept., 1972), 366–374.

The alternate view of science did come only after serious difficulties (anomalies) were discovered in the deductive-nomological account. Although Kuhn might avoid this charge by replying that his generalizations about science, paradigms, and paradigm-shifts do not refer to themselves, the difficulty that Scheffler has uncovered also exists on the level on which Kuhn does purport to speak, namely the acceptance or rejection of actual theories by scientists. On what basis do scientists accept or reject a new theory? If it cannot be on the basis of factual evidence, and if theories are incommensurable with one another, then how can a scientist ever seriously consider a new theory? He cannot reject the old theory until he has accepted the new one, for Kuhn claims that abandoning one paradigm occurs simultaneously with the adoption of a new one and how can this happen when one cannot understand a paradigm unless he has already adopted it? Kuhn seems caught in a contradiction when he both claims that there are competing paradigms and that paradigms are incommensurable. To adopt both of these requirements would force the scientist to make a blind jab into the future when he adopted a new paradigm, for there would be no way in which he could consider the old and the new paradigm together. The two paradigms would be incommensurable and one could not appeal to empirical evidence that was neutral with respect to both. Choosing a new paradigm would be highly subjective and highly whimsical, if possible at all. The notion of incommensurability underlies these contradictions. It seems to mean that there are sufficiently many words with different meanings in both theories such that the one cannot be understood in terms of the other.[41] When two theories are incommensurable, they cannot be alternatives. It can also be argued that theories like Darwin's and Kelvin's accounts of the age of the earth can be incommensurable and incompatible but need not be alternatives.[42]

That theories change and the situations in which they exist, the paradigms of Kuhn, also change is widely acknowledged. But how the change takes place and whether such changes can be explained rationally

41. Even this description of incommensurable is circular for we presume to know the meanings of each set of terms before we can judge that they are different. I am, however, indebted to J. N. Hattiangadi for the suggestion of it in his, "Alternatives and Incommensurables: The Case of Darwin and Kelvin," *Philosophy of Science*, 38, no. 4 (1971), 502–507.
42. Ibid.

and objectively does receive widespread debate. Due to the way that he has portrayed paradigms and paradigm-shifts, change seems either impossible or highly subjective on Kuhn's view. Kuhn has vigorously denied that his interpretation of science is irrational or subjective.[43] Yet, he also has not overcome these difficulties that plague his views on paradigm-shifts. Lakatos has attempted to solve these problems by offering an account of scientific change based upon research programs that progress by methodological falsification.[44] Such programs have a hard core set of irrefutable propositions (called by Lakatos a negative heuristic) which cannot be falsified. A protective belt of refutable propositions surrounds this hard core. Thus, theories can be compared by testing propositions derived from their protective belts. Usually, these tests do not result in crucial experiments. The hard cores of two theories, however, are not comparable and seem to be incommensurable in Kuhn's sense. Alternative theories compete with one another and the ones that generate testable hypotheses can be said to be progressing while those that are not fruitful in proposing hypotheses for empirical tests are said to be degenerating. After a time, research programs that are progressing lead us to accept the theory from which they are derived and we reject competitors that are degenerating.

In spite of Lakatos's claim that the acceptance of progressing research programs explains the rationality and the objectivity of how scientific theories change, there are examples like Copernicus and Einstein which defy classification as progressive research programs. Lakatos has stressed the need to adopt some empirical basis for the acceptance of theories, but his own effort is not fully successful, in part because he does not show how all parts of the theory are related to the observational procedures.

As an alternative to Hempel, Kuhn's proposed division of science into normal and revolutionary phases supported by the notion of a paradigm goes too far in stressing the subjective and nonrational elements of science. Scientists do compare theories and they do depend upon empirical evidence as a source of information that will assist them in deciding

43. Thomas S. Kuhn, "Postscript—1969," in *The Structure of Scientific Revolutions*, second edition; and "Reflections on my Critics," in *Criticism and the Growth of Knowledge*.

44. Imre Lakatos, "Falsification and the Methodology of Scientific Research Programmes," in *Criticism and the Growth of Knowledge*.

which theory to accept and which to reject. Much of the difficulty that Kuhn encounters arises from his assertion that all observation terms are theory-laden. Theories inform the investigator about what to look for and in what units to measure the phenomenon. Even the measuring instruments are constructed upon the basis of theoretical considerations. If theories determine the meaning of terms within them, then when a theory changes the meaning of the terms within it will change also. This is the notion of meaning variance and, as we have seen, leads to incommensurability of theories. But with meaning variance come certain paradoxes. With the same terms meaning different things in two different theories, falsification of statements derived from one theory by statements derived from the other becomes impossible. Even more severe is the problem of intelligibility. How can one come to understand a new theory when the terms in it have a meaning different from that which they had in the old theory? We cannot comprehend the new theory until we know the meaning of the terms in it and, yet, we cannot know the meanings of those terms until we understand the theory since the theory determines their meaning. Two major considerations about scientific language arise from the debate over the nature of scientific explanation: (1) what is the relationship between theoretical and observation terms? and (2) what is the nature of meaning variance? The first problem confronted the deductive account of explanation since the explanandum was assumed to be confirmable by observation statements independent of the logical conjunction of universal laws with initial conditions. In the view of science that stresses the change of scientific theories, the presumption that all observation terms were theoretical in origin eliminated the possibility of having empirical statements that were neutral with respect to theories. The problems of meaning variance were created by those like Kuhn, and especially Feyerabend, who rejected the cumulative aspect of science and insisted upon change as a basic feature of scientific explanation. In what follows, we shall examine both of these interrelated problems primarily not with an eye towards offering a better account of scientific explanation, for that is not our major purpose, but in an effort to discover some of the characteristics of scientific language that we shall later compare and contrast to religious language.

Consider again Boyle's discovery of the gas law $P_1V_1 = P_2V_2$ at constant temperature. Using a "J" tube with the long side of the tube open and the short side closed, Boyle added mercury to the longer side and noted the height in both arms of the tube. What he actually saw was the level of mercury and yet he could call it a measure of pressure since he could compute the volume of the tube and he knew the pressure of the atmosphere as that pressure which would support 29.5 inches of mercury. Adding mercury beyond 29.5 inches merely added the weight of the mercury to that of air pressure. Now the question arises as to what Boyle really observed. Did he observe pressure or did he merely observe the levels of mercury and then interpret them as pressure in light of his law? Kuhn, Feyerabend, and others would claim that Boyle observed pressure since they assert that all terms are theory-laden. Defenders of a neutral observation language argue that what Boyle saw was only the height of two columns of mercury and then, using the gas law, interpreted them as pressure. That these different ways of describing observations are not trivial can be seen in the consequences of each. Along with the claim that observations are theory-laden comes the assertion that theories cannot be compared by observation statements that are independent of them. Two theories cannot be compared, therefore, by how well they fit the data, for each theory prescribes independently and differently what the data will be and how to measure it. Proponents of theory-neutral observation statements argue that the very basis for objectivity is intersubjective testability and that commonsense observations of empirical phenomena do in fact take place. Furthermore, without such intersubjective tests, science would degenerate into a form of idealism where no empirical tests could alter the concepts generated by theories.

Both views of observation statements are extremes. Neither those who argue that since all observations are theory-laden, there cannot be any empirical tests independent of that theory, nor those who argue that all observation statements must be completely theory-neutral in order to insure objectivity can make their cases fully. Before Boyle formulated his gas law, when he was trying to refute Linus's funiculus theory, he observed levels of mercury. After the gas law, he observed the pressure of mercury and most of us today, when we look at a mercury barometer, read the height of the column of mercury as so many inches of *air pressure*. Corroboration of the gas laws has led us to use categories derived from them historically as categories for our observations. When Boyle first formulated his hypothesis about the relationship between pressure and volume, his theoretical statements involved pressure and his observation statements involved the height of mercury. With success, the category used for theory became that used to express observations. Grover Maxwell concludes that the difference between theoretical and observation terms is accidental, dependent upon our scientific knowledge and instrumentation available.[45] Note also that the original observation in Boyle's experiment, the measurement of length, was theory-neutral *with respect* to the gas law that was later formed on the basis of inductive generalization from the data. To be sure, measuring length depends upon theory, the theory of rigid rods, etc. But the theory upon which the measurement of the columns of mercury depends differs from the gas law theory. Mary Hesse rightly objects to the claim that no observations can be made independent of a theory for while she agrees that all observations are theory-laden, the theory upon which this particular observation statement depends need not be the theory for which it is an empirical test.[46] An observation statement that is dependent upon one theory may be neutral with regard to another. Hesse likens the relationship between theory and observation to a network of interrelated statements some of which can be considered theoretical when considered in the context of one theory while the same statements can be considered observational when considered in the context of another theory. Such a view denies both that theory and observation can be separated absolutely and that no tests independent of a given theory can be made.

Israel Scheffler defends the possibility of objective control over observation by suggesting that even though all observations are categorized, these categories may be revised when observations are made that clash with expected hypotheses.[47] Although he does not spell this out in detail, such clashes would only be possible where the categories of the observa-

45. Grover Maxwell, "The Ontological Status of Theoretical Entities," *Minnesota Studies in the Philosophy of Science*, vol. 3, pp. 14–15.

46. Mary Hesse, "Is There an Independent Observation Language?" in *The Nature and Function of Scientific Theories*, vol. 4, *University of Pittsburgh Series in the Philosophy of Science*, ed. Robert Colodny (Pittsburgh: University of Pittsburgh Press, 1970).

47. Israel Scheffler, *Science and Subjectivity*, ch. 2.

tion were derived from a theory different from the one that produced the hypothesis under consideration. Kuhn did not allow for this possibility when he argued that whereas Priestly saw dephlogisticated air, Lavoisier saw oxygen. From a theory neutral to both theories, one could say that each man observed a gas and then tested that observation against his theoretical expectations. When the measurements of the quantity of that gas repeatedly confirmed Lavoisier's predictions, he claimed that the gas that he observed was oxygen. The fact that we do not always discover in experiments what we expect to find becomes possible when we remember that although all observations are theory-laden, the observations that will confirm or disconfirm statements derived from this particular theory, may be theory-neutral with respect to the same particular theory under consideration. Kuhn and others have failed to recognize that observation statements loaded by one theory may be independent of another theory.

The view that since all observations are theory-laden, the observations of this theory must be loaded by this theory can lead to some peculiar results. Hanson wrote that Tycho and Kepler observed different "suns" since they held different theories of plantary motion.[48] Yet visual or telescopic observation of the sun depended upon neither theory of the solar system. In addition, both astronomers could have predicted locations for the planets upon the basis of their theory, and then these could have been tested against observation of the sun or the projections for the particular planet. To object to such a comparison on the grounds that "sun" has different theoretical considerations in each theory is to forget that in terms of visual observation, the same sun appears to both observers. Kordig in an interesting analysis argues that Hanson's mistake arises from his equation of "seeing that" and "believing that."[49] He cites examples showing that it can be possible for observers to hold contradictory beliefs about the same object.

The relativity of the distinction between theory and observation does not make observations independent of a particular theory, for even though all observations are theory-laden, the ones pertinent to this theory may be dependent upon another theory. This is not to underestimate the

48. Norwood Russell Hanson, *Patterns of Discovery*, ch. 1.
49. Carl R. Kordig, *The Justification of Scientific Change* (Dordrecht, Holland: Reidel, 1971), ch. 1, "The Theory-ladenness of Observation."

degree to which theories do determine the nature of measurement in experiment. When we test for volts, we expect to read volts on a volt-meter and not pressure. In a very real sense, especially well-confirmed theories do generate observation tests that are loaded by that theory. But in scientific situations where new speculative hypotheses are under test, there must be the possibility of independent confirmation and such demands draw upon the skill of the researcher to formulate experiments that will provide the kind of objective test that can stand the scrutiny of his peers. Theory and observation are parts of the same network of statements and relative to what theory is under consideration. The positivist's dream of two distinct levels of language has long faded in the opaque boundary between observation and theory.

The interrelationship between theory and experiment is vividly de-monstrated by the discovery of the positron.[50] Although in 1931 Dirac had predicted an electronic particle with positive charge, and had decided that the proton would not do since its mass was too large, when Carl Anderson first experimentally identified a positive electron on August 2, 1932, he was unable to show that this was the particle predicted by Dirac. Anderson was unfamiliar with Dirac's work and, when confronted with a strange new particle track, he was unable to explain its presence. While identifying it as a positive electronic particle, Anderson was puzzled as to how it could occur and why other researchers had not also found it. Only shortly thereafter, when Blackett and Occhialini had developed a new technique for photographing particle tracks, were they able to equate the particle found by Anderson with that theoretically predicted by Dirac. In this observation, the experimental results and theoretical prediction were welded into one particle, the positron. In Dirac's theory, a few of the quantum states of negative kinetic energy are unoccupied by electrons and, instead, are filled with particles of positive kinetic energy and positive charge, namely, positrons. When showers of these positrons occur, they quickly disappear as they react with readily available negative electrons to form two or more quanta of energy. This latter fact explains why so few early experimenters had encountered positrons. Probably, as scrutiny of earlier photographic plates seems to indicate, some research-

50. Norwood Russell Hanson, *The Concept of the Positron* (Cambridge: Cambridge University Press, 1963).

ers did record tracks of particles that we now know as positrons, but they did not "observe" positrons in the sense of knowing what they were seeing. In order to do that, they would have had to know what to expect and this could only have been provided by a theoretical prediction. It is significant that in the discovery of the positron we have clearcut evidence of a theoretical term becoming an observation term. What was predicted by Dirac was discovered by Blackett and Occhialini. Anderson had merely found evidence of an unusual positively charged particle, but he really did not know what he had uncovered.

From the perspective of the cumulative view of science, positivists had assumed that scientific terms retained the same meaning when they were used in a new theory. This constancy of meaning allowed statements derived from a later theory to contradict statements generated by an earlier theory since the same terms appearing in both theories were considered to be meaning invariant. Under the new view of science, however, scientific terms were thought to derive their meaning from the theory in which they resided so that a change in theories also meant a change in the meanings of the terms appearing in those theories. No longer could statements derived from theories be falsified. Theories were viewed as incommensurable with each other since the meaning of even the same terms in each were different. And historians of science provided copious evidence that meanings of scientific terms do change. Consider, for instance, the terms, "atom" and "force."

Democritus, seeking an ultimate explanation of change, was one of the first to suggest that the world was composed of an infinite number of irreducible particles, called "atoms," of different sizes and shapes, but qualitatively identical.[51] All of these "atoms" were in motion. Although the concept was supplanted by Aristotle's mechanics and metaphysics, Descartes reaffirmed it when he posited a world filled with moving particles of differing degrees of coarseness in his vortex theory of motion. Newton gave a much different account of motion, but retained the notion of a world composed of corpuscular particles ("atoms"). These particles conformed to the Newtonian laws of motion and were, therefore, deter-

51. Andrew G. Van Melsen, *From Atmos to Atom: The History of the Concept Atom*, tr. Henry J. Koren (Pittsburgh: Duquesne University Press, 1952).

minate. The concept of the atom took a radical turn in the modern period when John Dalton in the nineteenth century associated it with the weights of chemical elements. Avogadro helped the concept of the atom along by showing how atoms could combine into molecules. When "atoms" and "molecules" were employed in the kinetic theory of gases, some scientists began to think of these concepts as possessing their own "reality." Objections were immediately raised by those like Ernst Mach who wanted the concept to remain as a part of a mathematical model with no objective reality of its own.

Next, the concept moved from the mechanical to the electrical realm as atoms were linked with electrons. Atoms now possessed not only mass and motion, but a charge as well. Electrical energy was transmitted from atom to atom by electromagnetic waves. H. Lorentz developed the concept even further by arguing that the analogous wave motion of both light and electricity plus the experimental evidence of incandescence meant that the electrons of the atom were responsible for the emission of light. The concept, however, still remained within the context of a mechanical theory as atoms were considered to be irreducible solid objects having additional properties (electronic, light, etc.).

The Rutherford-Bohr model of the atom marked a transition from the notions of classical mechanics to modern quantum theory. The visual model for the atom was the solar system, with the electron orbiting around the nucleus. Both the nucleus and the electrons were interpreted as solid particles. However, to account for the fact that electrons circling the nucleus would emit energy and eventually the atom would wear down contrary to experimental evidence, Bohr postulated stable orbits in which electrons would not lose energy. Only when they jumped from one orbit to another (quantum leaps) would there be a change in energy. The beauty of Bohr's model was that it accounted for the periodic table of chemical elements.

Another analogy, that between the wave-particle duality of light and similar properties in the atom, led Louis de Broglie in 1924 to assert mathematically that equations describing both particles and waves were applicable to the atom. And so the era of the contemporary atom dawned. Splitting the nucleus brought about the end of the notion of irreducibility. Out of the nucleus came a host of additional particles, protons, neutrinos, mesons, positrons, etc. Through the bombardment of the nucleus, interactions among particles and transmutations have been observed with the emission and absorption of energy. No longer could conservation of mass be maintained as a physical law; in its place came the law of the conservation of energy. Dividing the atom was like opening Pandora's Box out of which sprang so many particles that a stable picture of the atom seems, at present, highly unlikely. The future may hold a simple model of the atom, but if the history of the concept is any guide to its further development, then it is unlikely.

One of the striking things about the changes in the meaning of the term "atom" is that in each transition it has been used as a metaphor. When scientists wanted to build a new theory about the atom, they took the old term with its old associations and gave it new properties. In the mechanical theory, new properties like its electrical nature were added to the old term. When the shift in meaning was considerable, as in the Rutherford-Bohr theory, an analogy of the planets circling the sun was used as a model to describe the activity within the atom. When seeking to propose an hypothesis about the atom, scientists extended the meaning of the term by suggesting new features either by analogy or by adding new properties. To use a known linguistic expression to stand for the unknown is the primary characteristic of a metaphor.

That the term "force" was also used as a metaphor can be seen by looking briefly at the different meanings that it has had from Newton to the present.[52] Even Newton himself held different views of "force." He thought that the concept was both the innate "force" of momentum and the impressed "force" of motion, concepts which are not consistent with each other. It is also fairly well known that Newton's gravitational "force" is inconsistent with his laws of motion. Many contemporary textbooks treat Newton's second law of motion ($f=ma$) as if it were a precise definition, but Newton clearly distinguished between definitions and axioms, relegating the second law to the latter rather than the former. Newton probably took the "force" of the second law to be a concept given intuitively by analogy to man's muscular "force." In any event,

52. Max Jammer, *Concepts of Force: A Study in the Foundations of Dynamics* (New York: Harper Torchbooks, 1962).

Newton certainly held to several different concepts of "force" of which that in the second law is only one.

Since Newton, there has been an effort by scientists to eliminate the term "force" as an unnecessary concept. Mach, Kirchhoff, and Hertz were all of this mind. In contemporary physics, "force" plays the role of an intermediate methodological term and, although possessing little explantory power, is still used in statics and dynamics. Quantum mechanics, by using the terms of classical mechanics, has also kept "force" as a device for economy of thought, based upon analogy with the human body. General relativity has led to a revision of the concept, but this is presently in a confused state and the process is by no means complete.

The indefinite status that "force" has come to have in quantum mechanics and relativity should not surprise us as these theories are fundamentally different from classical mechanics and we would expect terms appropriate to the old theory to have a different status in these new theories. But Newton's ambiguous and metaphorical use of the term "force" does catch us unawares.[53] For those who have assumed that Newtonian mechanics was a paradigm of logical rigor and a model for how scientists should construct theories, it is absolutely shocking! For too long, the fantasy has persisted that science uses a well defined, precise, and unambiguous language. These illusions were harbored by those positivists who believed that science was cumulative and scientific explanation based upon the deductive-nomological account.

Although scientists strived for precision in the expression of their theories, at least some were aware that the imprecision of language necessarily hampered their efforts. Werner Heisenberg, formulator of the Uncertainty Principle, noted the difficulty of "talking" about contemporary science since the ordinary words that we possess are often rooted in a commonsense understanding of the world and are not applicable to quantum theory.

The most difficult problem, however, concerning the use of the language arises in quantum theory. Here we have at first no simple guide for correlating the mathematical symbols with concepts of

53. J. E. McGuire, "Transmutation and Immutability: Newton's Doctrine of Physical Qualities," *Ambix*, 14, no. 2 (June, 1967).

ordinary language; and the only thing we know from the start is the fact that our common concepts cannot be applied to the structure of the atoms.[54]

Other scientists as well as philosophers of science have similarly noted the use of metaphor in science.[55] Too often, however, metaphors have been thought of as undesirable substitutes for precise definitions. They were thought to be the primary possession of poets who wished to dream about the world rather than to explain it in a theory. The very nature of science, however, is such that scientists need the metaphor as a bridge between old and new theories. Only by some such device as a metaphor is it possible to develop new meanings in new theories that are intelligible. Metaphors have a hypothetical nature; they suggest possible new meanings to us. In attempting to describe the unknown, the scientist must use terms that are known to us. Sometimes this is done mathematically, but often ordinary words are stretched in their meanings to accomodate new hypothetical understandings. When concepts are applied to empirical cases, there may well be not only an imprecision in measurement, but also an inexactitude in conceptualization.[56]

When scientists employ metaphors to suggest new meanings in new theories, they offer us a way of avoiding the paradox of unintelligibility that many philosophers see resulting from the problem of meaning variance.[57] A metaphor results from the juxtaposition of the old and the new. Our familiarity with the old usage allows us to recognize the terms as meaningful while the new usage suggests a different way of comprehending its meaning.[58] If we find the new meaning significant, then we

54. Werner Heisenberg, *Physics and Philosophy* (New York: Harper Torchbooks, 1958), p. 177.

55. Cf. Mary Hesse, *Models and Analogies in Science* (Notre Dame: University of Notre Dame Press, 1966), p. 170; Ernest H. Hutten, *The Language of Modern Physics* (London: Allen & Unwin, 1956).

56. Cf. D. H. Mellor, "Experimental Error and Deducibility," *Philosophy of Science*, 32, no. 2 (April, 1965), 105–122; "Inexactness and Explanation," *Philosophy of Science*, 33, no. 4 (Dec., 1966), 345–359; "Imprecision and Explanation," *Philosophy of Science*, 34, no. 1 (March, 1967), 1–9.

57. Peter Achinstein, "On the Meaning of Scientific Terms," *Journal of Philosophy*, 61, no. 17 (Sept. 17, 1964), 497–509.

58. Earl R. MacCormac, "Meaning Variance and Metaphor," *British Journal for the Philosophy of Science*, 22 (1971), 145–159. I will show how this is possible in more detail in chapter 3 when I deal with metaphor.

drop the older meaning associated with the term. Without the possibility of proposing new hypothetical meanings, science could not create new theories. And without the possibility of formulating such new hypotheses by extending the meanings of terms that we already comprehend, science could not produce new theories that are intelligible.

By considering the debate over the nature of scientific explanation among philosophers of science, we have identified several major features of scientific language. Contrary to the assumptions of early positivisitic philosophers, theoretical terms cannot be reduced to observation terms. The line between observation and theory becomes extremely difficult to draw since all observation terms are dependent upon theoretical considerations for their meaning. But this does not turn science into a subjective enterprise in which anyone can posit a theory that finds inevitable confirmation because the theory determines the nature of the observation terms. Observation terms can be neutral with respect to a particular theory even though they may be dependent upon another theory for their meaning.

Without this possibility, objectivity would be impossible. Theory and observation can be properly viewed as a network of interrelated statements where some of the nodes of the intersections are grounded in empirical observation for a particular theory. For another theory, different nodes will become the places at which observation statements are confirmed or disconfirmed. Just as it was impossible to reduce all theoretical terms to observation terms, so it becomes equally impossible to reduce all observation terms to theoretical terms. What are observation terms in one context may become theoretical terms in another.

The second and third features of scientific terms are closely related. Many scientific terms are imprecise and ambiguous because they suggest hypothetical speculations about new and unexplored phenomena. For those who believed that scientific explanation could be understood largely in terms of logic, the acknowledgement that numerous scientific terms are not well defined comes as a blow that severely damages the notion that science proceeds by deductive inference. A large number of these imprecise scientific terms are metaphors: familiar terms used in unusual ways to suggest new meanings. And the scientist needs the metaphor to express his hypotheses in an intelligible manner, for without it, he would be unable to construct new theories that are radically different from traditional theories. The scientific revolutions since the seventeenth century attest to the radical shifts in meanings that have taken place, and historical studies of scientific terms clearly demonstrate the metaphoric character of many terms. In coining new terms, scientists are like poets, but as we shall see when we consider the nature of metaphor more fully, the kinds of metaphors that scientists use are not purely suggestive, as are many of those used by poets. Before pursuing the nature of scientific metaphor more carefully, we shall turn our attention to another type of metaphoric language, religious language, that has been measured philosophically by the standards of meaning developed in the philosophy of science.

II

The nature of religious language

In the twentieth century, philosophers of religion have been concerned to determine whether an adequate justification can be given which will demonstrate that religious language is meaningful. Doubts that religious language was meaningful had been raised by positivists using the principle of verification as their criterion for meaning. Since religious language was neither tautologous nor capable of simple empirical verification, it was declared meaningless. Although devoid of meaning, religious utterances were thought to express the sentiments and emotional feelings of believers. Even though men might agree upon their feelings and band together in groups, such feelings could never be construed as genuine knowledge because sentiments lacked a cognitive status. Under the positivist interpretation, therefore, religious belief was based upon noncognitive feelings, a nonrational, if not irrational, foundation.

Those who considered religious language to be nonsense also assumed that, by contrast, scientific language was the epitome of meaningful discourse. The language of scientists could be tested by simple experiments in which publicly observable events could be agreed upon by a multitude of witnesses. And the abstract nonobservable parts of theories were composed of tautologous mathematical relations and theoretical terms that could be reduced to observable terms by logical methods that also prohibited the introduction of metaphysical or religious terms into the language. The positivist description of science went even further in specifying the differences between scientific and religious language. While scientific explanations were composed of precise events deduced from a conjunction of initial conditions and laws expressible in logical form, religious descriptions of the world depended upon nonrational associations of imprecise ideas from which no testable events could be deduced. Theologians were faulted not only for failing to present a deductive account that could be empirically tested, but also for employing a language that lacked precision. The prevalence of metaphor in religious discourse was taken to be confirmation that religious language failed utterly as a legitimate mode of meaningful communication.[1] And when metaphors degenerated into myths, philosophers demanding verification were absolutely convinced that religious language was meaningless, for myths were acknowledged even by theologians to be imaginary stories that could never be empirically confirmed.

The early debate about the meaning of religious language followed very closely developments in the philosophy of science. Standards, used to justify the meaningfulness of scientific language, were then applied by positivists to religious language with seemingly shattering effect. When verifiability was in vogue as the method by which scientists were presumed to confirm their predictions, the demand was made that if religious language was to be considered meaningful, it must be shown to be verifiable. And theologians responded to the challenge by developing a number of apologies purporting to show that religious discourse could be verified in principle. When the principle of verifiability was abandoned by philosophers in favor of falsifiability, theologians responded again, this time trying to demonstrate the falsifiability of their statements. Seldom did theologians or philosophers of religion pay close attention to the details of the discussions over falsifiability and confirmation that took place in the philosophy of science itself. In each case, the criterion of meaning proposed by positivists and empiricists was lifted out of the context in the philosophy of science where it was under discussion and applied in a simplistic manner to religious language. Unmitigated demands were made of religious language that scientific language never could have fulfilled. As we shall see shortly, if the same demands had been made of scientific language that had been made of religious discourse, scientific language would have been shown to have been as meaningless as religious language. Both critics of and apologists for religious language debated its meaningfulness on the basis of erroneous assumptions about the nature of scientific language. In contrast to religious language which they believed to be ambiguous and difficult to verify (or falsify) directly,

1. Paul Edwards, "Professor Tillich's Confusions," *Mind*, 74 (April, 1965), 192–214.

they assumed that scientific language was unambiguous and easy to test by direct verification (or falsification).

A second type of debate about how to justify the meaningfulness of religious language took place upon the assumption that the indictment of religious language based upon the criteria for meaning used in the philosophy of science was illegitimate. Many contemporary theologians were not surprised at all when religious language was found to be either unverifiable or unfalsifiable for they had never assumed that philosophical criteria applicable to science were also applicable to religion. On the contrary, they presumed that science and religion were two distinct enterprises and that the context of each determined its own meaningfulness. These presumptions were reinforced by the long and desolatory war between science and religion over Darwin. Many theologians were convinced by that conflict that they ought never to tread upon the soil occupied by science again and that their best hope for survival rested upon as complete a separation of the two camps as possible.

In spite of the tranquility of the separation, a number of philosophers of religion and philosophical theologians felt compelled to offer a linguistic defense for this division into different realms of meaning. Since the later Wittgenstein had argued for viewing language not as a single universal essence with fixed meanings, but rather as a multiplicity of language usages each meaning of which is determined by its own context, defenders of the separation of religious from scientific language found in Wittgenstein a basis for their apology. Religious language could be viewed under their interpretation as a special language game, the rules of which were determined by the context of the religious situation. Although an odd language by ordinary standards, religious language could be seen as meaningful within the context of religion itself. And there were certain parallels between religious usage and the use of ordinary language that supported the belief that religious language merely took ordinary words and properly infused them with new meanings according to a set of common experiences. Convictional statements whether of ordinary discourse, or as used by believers, had a similar logical form. The analysis of first-person discourse provided another link between common language and the religious use of language.

The whole defense of religious language on the ground of separate contexts of meaning avoided the challenges of verifiability and falsifiability, but only on the belief that religious language could not and *should* not meet these demands. The notion that religious language cannot find empirical confirmation in a manner similar to scientific language was always lurking in the background as an assumption for those who sought to demonstrate that a Wittgensteinian defense could serve to justify religious discourse.

Our approach to considering the nature of religious language will be to examine first the debates over the meaningfulness of religious language based upon the demands for verification and falsification, and those based upon a belief that scientific and religious languages should be separated. In each case, our examination of the arguments will be constructed in light of what we have discovered about the nature of scientific language in the preceding chapter. Then, we shall turn our attention briefly to a number of pronouncements about the nature of religious language that have been made outside the debate over its meaningfulness. Finally, drawing upon some parallels between religious and scientific language, we shall present our own description of the nature of religious language.

The demand that a statement must be verifiable takes as its paradigm the observation statement. When one says (1) "The only table in this room is wooden, rectangular, and green," this statement is verifiable in the sense that we can look and see whether or not there is in fact a table in this room and whether it possesses the properties of being "wooden," "rectangular" and "green." We do not have to carry out the actual verification for the statement to be meaningful; we must be able to observe the object for it to be verifiable. Nor must the verification turn out to yield a true statement for many false statements are quite meaningful. Even if (1) turns out to be false upon inspection of the table in this room, we can still count (1) as meaningful for by the positivist's criterion of verifiability, we know how to test for its truth or falsity and that is what gives meaning to it.

That much religious language cannot be verified by direct observation seems fairly obvious. "God" in the statement "God exists" cannot be seen in the way that a green, wooden, rectangular table can be seen. Illustrative of the unverifiability of religious discourse was John Wisdom's famous parable of the unweeded garden.[2] Two men come upon a long neglected garden with which they were once familiar. Although there are many weeds, a few plants survive in good form. One man remarks that a gardener must have taken care of the garden while they were absent. They check with neighbors and find that to their knowledge, no one has been there. The first man persists and still claims that a gardener was there, suggesting, perhaps, that he worked while people slept. This hypothesis is eliminated by the second man who points out that someone would have heard him if he had worked at night. The first man then asserts that the gardener must be "unseen" and "unheard," in fact, invisible. The second man says that no gardener, visible or invisible, comes, for look at the weeds and the neglect of the garden. Still, the first man persists, tenaciously showing the skeptic bits of evidence of order in the garden. Wisdom asks if the dispute can be settled by investigation of the garden and, of course, tells us that it cannot. The beliefs of the two men regarding the presence of a gardener are more indicative of their feelings about the garden than they are about its actual state of repair, for both agree on the existence of the weeds and the plants. No evidence that the skeptic could present from the state of the garden (world) would convince the believer that the invisible gardener (God) was not responsible for it.

Apologists who took the demand for verifiability seriously were well aware that religious statements could not be verified by direct public observation. They asserted, however, that human experience included more than just observation and that religious claims could be confirmed by religious experiences possessed by believers. After all, the church had always expressed its doctrines in terms of the common experiences of Christians. Whether it was sensing God's presence through the sacraments or through a reading of His word, these were experiences proclaimed by the faithful as evidence for their doctrinal statements. Acknowledging the critic's charge that such experiences are limited to believers and are not the possession of all men, apologists reply that religious experiences are like aesthetic experiences, not all men possess them, but all men are capable of achieving them through learning and practice. Although less universal than observations, religious experiences

2. John Wisdom, "Gods," reprinted in his *Philosophy and Psycho-Analysis* (Oxford: Basil Blackwell, 1957), pp. 149–168.

are professed by sizeable numbers and are claimed to be no less real than experiences of beauty or of love.

John Hick attempted to show that religious language was verifiable by appealing to the Christian doctrine of life after death.[3] Aware that beliefs about God are not capable of observational verification, Hick argues that indirect verification is possible by means of experiencing the fulfillment of God's purpose for ourselves and experiencing communion with God as revealed in Christ. Both of these goals can only be finally verified in the eschatological event of communion with God after death. This possibility of a future verification makes religious language verifiable and, therefore, meaningful. The psychological belief that religious statements will be verified in a future event protects religious language from the charge that it is unverifiable. And in no way can religious statements about God be falsified since their verification always remains in the future.

The program to show that there are factual claims in religious language that can be verified eschatologically was challenged by Kai Nielsen chiefly on the grounds that we must assume the existence of God in Hick's argument in order to show that the statement "God exists" is verifiable.[4] If faith in a future event guarantees the meaning of the term "God," then how can we have faith in "God" without first understanding something of the meaning of that term? Hick agrees that his argument based upon eschatological verification does not set forth the full truth-conditions of the statement "God exists," but he still maintains that his argument does show that "God exists" is factually true or false.[5] For conceiving of conditions under which verification could take place fulfills the demands of the positivist for a meaningful statement.

The debate about the verifiability of religious language has not persisted largely because philosophers of religion became aware of the logical faults of verification and the principle of falsification replaced it.[6] We have already seen that a universal hypothetical statement can never be

3. John Hick, "Theology and Verification," *Theology Today*, 17, no. 1 (April, 1960), 12–31; John Hick, *Faith and Knowledge*, second edition (Ithaca: Cornell University Press, 1966), pp. 186–199.
4. Kai Nielsen, "Eschatological Verification," *Canadian Journal of Theology*, 9, no. 4 (1963), 271–281.
5. John Hick, *Faith and Knowledge*, p. 197.
6. George I. Mavrodes argues this point in his "God and Verification," *Canadian Journal of Theology*, 10, no. 3 (1964), 187–191.

verified since a true consequent does not necessarily yield a true antecedent and since one usually cannot enumerate all of the confirming instances of that antecedent. In response to this shift in criterion for meaning, apologists for religion sought to justify religious language by showing that it was falsifiable, that is, capable of being falsified. For a religious statement to be meaningful, there had to be possible evidence that could count against it.

Probably the most influential discussion of this issue occurred in *University* under the title of "Theology and Falsification" and reprinted and widely read in *New Essays in Philosophical Theology*.[7] Antony Flew began the discussion by taking John Wisdom's parable of the invisible gardener and strengthening it by putting electrified barbed wire and dogs around the garden and showing how to persist in claiming "a gardener, invisible, intangible, insensible to electric shocks, a gardener who has not scent and makes not sound, a gardener who comes secretly to look after the garden which he loves," is to kill the assertion that there is a gardener by the death of "a thousand qualifications." In Flew's statement of the parable, each time the skeptic proposes a test to discover the gardener and it turns out negative, the believer modifies his concept of the gardener to exclude that particular test. The believer will allow no test to undermine his faith that the invisible gardener comes to tend the garden. Since such belief is unfalsifiable, Flew concludes that it is meaningless, for meaningful statements depend upon the possibility of finding a test that might falsify them.

Bettering the principle that one parable deserves another, R. M. Hare produced two in response to Flew.[8] Both involve a neologism, a "blik," which is a type of nonfalsifiable belief. The first parable involves a student convinced that his Oxford dons are out to murder him and no amount of good will can convince him to the contrary. The student possesses an insane "blik," but others who know that the dons are really not murderers at all possess a sane "blik." The second parable treats a "blik" about the properties of steel and one's confidence or lack of confidence in a steering-wheel. Hare asserts that these "bliks" affect our actions contrary

7. Antony Flew and Alasdair MacIntyre, eds., *New Essays in Philosophical Theology* (London: SCM Press, 1955).
8. Ibid., pp. 99–103.

to the state of the detached observers in the parable about the garden. Hare says in response to the challenge of falsification, that there are religious statements that are not falsifiable, but which are meaningful since they affect our everyday actions. Flew countered by arguing that "bliks" are really normative statements clothed with superfluous religious terms like "God."[9] He claimed that statements like "You ought *because* it is God's will" do little more than to assert that "You ought." Or, "My soul must be immortal *because* God loves his children . . . " expresses the statement "My soul must be immortal." By interpreting theological statements as unverifiable bliks, fixed ways of looking at the world that affect our actions in it, Flew believed that Hare had emptied such statements of all religious content.

Basil Mitchell met the challenge of falsification directly by contending against Flew that evidence like pain counts against the theological assertion "God is loving," but pain does not count *decisively* against it.[10] Articles of faith can be provisional hypotheses to be discarded when warranted by experience. Mitchell also objects to the "blik" as vacuous since no evidence could tell against it. He illustrates his distinction between evidence that counts against a theory and evidence that *decisively* counts against the same theory by a parable of a stranger among partisans in wartime believed to be the leader of the partisans who commits activities that could be interpreted both as evidence that he was not a partisan, when he aided the enemy for instance, and as evidence that he was working for the partisans since his seemingly treasonous actions could also be understood as done to cover his identity. Whether theological expressions can be falsified, then, depends upon whether there exists a real difference between "counting against" and "counting decisively against." In terms of the logic of falsification, no difference exists, but among scientists, as we have already noted, many laws and theories are adopted in spite of the existence of negative evidence. Philosophical theologians, however, did not develop this line of defense, for most of the literature on the falsifiability of religious language deals with the problem on the level of affirming or denying that individual statements are falsifi-

9. Ibid., pp. 106–108, and cf. Paul M. van Buren, *The Secular Meaning of the Gospel* (London: SCM Press, 1963).
10. *New Essays in Philosophical Theology*, pp. 103–105.

able.[11] By proceeding in this manner, the demand for falsifiability posed a dilemma for the theological apologist. Either he could claim that his statements were falsifiable, but not in the same way that empirical ones were (bliks), which was hardly satisfying to empirically-minded philosophers, or he could deny that falsifiability was applicable to his assertions. The latter meant that the criterion of meaning for scientific statements was not applicable to religious discourse.

As in most dilemmas, the solution can be found by accepting neither horn of the dilemma and by reconstituting the problem. For when philosophers of religion adopted the principle of falsifiability as a criterion of meaning, they did so with little or no attention to its fate among philosophers of science. Naively, they assumed that each major religious utterance like "God exists" or "God is love" must be shown to be falsifiable in order to be adjudged meaningful. Although philosophers of science were tempted to do the same thing with individual scientific statements, it soon became apparent that falsification involved a network of assumptions and hypotheses and it was difficult to say just which part of that network had been falsified when negative evidence appeared.[12] The Duhem-Quine thesis asserts that any one part of a conjunction of empirical conditions and hypotheses may by false when an experiment turns out negative. Unless scientists adopt another theory, they usually develop auxiliary hypotheses to mitigate the negative evidence or they merely hold those results in abeyance until they can find a better explanation.

Much of the difficulty that defenders of religious language have had with both verifiability and falsifiability has resulted from their failure to distinguish between theoretical terms and terms that are either observable or experiential. Theologians do not expect the term "God" to be observable, yet they have allowed themselves to be drawn into a debate about whether the statement "God exists" can be falsified where

11. Cf. D. R. Duff-Forbes, "Theology and Falsification Again," *Australasian Journal of Philosophy*, 39, no. 2 (Aug., 1961), 143–154; more recently William Austin has suggested the use of Lakatos's notion of research programmes be applied to the problem of religious language, "Religious Commitment and the Logical Status of Doctrines," *Religious Studies*, 9, no. 1 (March, 1973), 39–48.

12. Lakatos, "Criticism and the Methodology of Scientific Research Programmes," *Proceedings of the Aristotelian Society* 69, (1968–1969) pp. 149–186.

falsification is construed as the observation of objects. The term "God" is highly abstract, ambiguous, and often metaphorical. Theologians and philosophers use it to describe a whole range of experiences and may attribute to it aspects of reality that are not directly testable. But to object to religion on the grounds that statements involving "God" are not falsifiable seems as absurd as objecting to science on the grounds that some theoretical terms cannot be directly tested. The term "God" forms an integral part of a series of relations and beliefs that find confirmation or disconfirmation in human experience. Men do lose their faith when adversity strikes while others persist through the same events. This means that falsifiability is much more complex in religion than in science, for there are more human variables involved. It is also much more subjective for the same experience may be interpreted in different ways according to the varying beliefs of those doing the interpretation. Yet, the events that we experience are interpreted in the light of our theoretical beliefs. We have already seen that observation statements determined by one theory may be neutral with respect to another theory. Certainly, religious statements are determined by beliefs that are very much like theoretical statements so that when a believer interprets his experience, he does so in light of his religious doctrines. When his religious expectations are not fulfilled in his daily life and he encounters evidence that would count against his beliefs, he may still hold those beliefs, as Mitchell suggested, by denying that such falsifications count decisively against his religion. His faith continues in spite of adversity, or he may formulate auxiliary hypotheses to explain why he has encountered the adversity. Whether religious statements informed by one set of beliefs can be neutral with respect to another set of beliefs will have to be explored more carefully. We shall do so after we have considered other types of apology for the meaningfulness of religious language. For the present, we can conclude that relatively few religious statements need to find confirmation in human experience since very many doctrinal claims do not result in statements that can be examined empirically. Religious experience does affect the nature of beliefs but, conversely, the very character of the experience and the way in which we describe it is determined by theological doctrines. If theology found no confirmation in observable human actions, then the charge that it was meaningless or nonsense could easily be sustained. But to claim, as those who first demanded verification or falsification for religious discourse did, that basic religious statements like "God exists" must be testable empirically, ignores the character of confirmation itself. Only a very few statements derived from a scientific theory can be confirmed by observation and the theory may persist as a legitimate theory even when some negative data accumulates. Similarly, in theology only a very few statements derived from a system of beliefs can result in actions that are observable and these actions are necessarily interpreted in light of the religious beliefs of the actor. In both cases, the possibility of inventing auxiliary hypotheses to explain negative events makes the job of falsification enormously difficult.

Many theologians, however, were convinced that the criteria of meaning that justified scientific language did not properly apply to religious language. In contrast to the statements of science that were confirmed by observations, expressions of personal convictions gave religious statements their truth-value. These theologians were not at all surprised that apologists could not demonstrate the verifiability or the falsifiability of religious discourse. Religious discourse, they argued, differed significantly from the utterances of science and to judge the meaning or truth of the former by the standards of the latter was to commit a fundamental mistake.

Much of the explication and philosophical defense of this interpretation stressing the difference of religious and scientific language depended upon the notions of language that Wittgenstein had developed in his *Philosophical Investigations*.[13] In his earlier *Tractatus Logico Philosophicus*, Wittgenstein had argued that language, in the form of a symbolic logic, mirrors or pictures the world and that any utterance incapable of such representation is nonsense.[14] This early program of Wittgenstein set aside religious language as inexpressible. By the time the *Philosophical Investigations* was finished, he had changed his mind drastically about the nature of language. No longer did Wittgenstein affirm a single universal essence for language; instead he viewed language as a collection of different usages. The context of each language use determined the rules by

13. Ludwig Wittgenstein, *Philosophical Investigations*, tr. by G. E. M. Anscombe, third edition (Oxford: Basil Blackwell, 1968).
14. Ludwig Wittgenstein, *Tractatus Logico Philosophicus*, tr. D. Pears and B. McGuiness (Oxford: Basil Blackwell, 1961).

which meaning could be interpreted. He coined his famous phrase "language game" to describe the contextual aspect of linguistic usage. Men play various language games with the rules of each determined by the nature of the game itself. The many language games shared a family of resemblances so that communication among the variety of games was possible. This analysis of language offered philosophers of religion anxious to stress the differences between scientific and religious language a ready-made platform upon which to erect a defense of their interpretation. Under this view, science and religion could be interpreted as different language games with different rules determining meaning and truth within each. The application of the rules for scientific language to religious language mistakenly assumed that these two language games were one.

Wittgenstein was well aware that men do misuse language; in fact, he described the task of the philosopher in terms of a therapist who relieved mental cramps caused by the misuse of language. But, what is misuse? How can we tell when we are using language properly? Wittgenstein suggested that proper use consisted in a description of how people ordinarily use a term and this is the usual interpretation given to his pronouncement. He was aware, however, that one cannot just record what people say for in many cases that would be repeating improper usage and the philosopher must correct that, so he resorted to the invention of examples that are contrary to our intuitions about language. Usually the proper use is discovered only when one has imagined what it would be like for the use to be otherwise, or what are the possible consequences of such a use that one might not have acknowledged.[15] Now this distinction between proper use and misuse raises an interesting question about religious language. Is it a proper use justified as a language game or is it a misuse arising from the improper use of ordinary language? Critics condemned religious language as a confused and odd use of ordinary language that can be corrected by eliminating the theological ascriptions of "supernatural" or "transcendent" to terms like "father." Defenders claimed that religious discourse, although different from the ordinary use of language, was not odd or illegitimate since its

15. Cf. Earl R. MacCormac, "Wittgenstein's Imagination," *Southern Journal of Philosophy*, 10, no. 4 (Winter, 1972), 453–461.

unusual usages were analogous to certain forms of ordinary talk that were often overlooked by critics. Two of the forms of ordinary use used as analogies to theological language were first person or I-talk and statements of "belief in" or "trust in" another person.

Statements about God are like first person convictional statements of the form "I believe in . . ." in a number of ways.[16] The first comes from the fact that there can be no objective way of testing such statements. If I say, "I believe in John" meaning that I trust him to do the right thing, I am stating a conviction that I may retain even if John does the wrong thing in this instance. Spokesmen for this position maintain that one cannot force convictional statements into categories of truth or falsity. Nor can one change every statement "I believe in . . ." into another of the form "I believe that . . ." for there is a vast difference between convictional statements expressing trust in persons or God and beliefs in propositions. "Belief that" always involves presuppositions of some factual propositions. When one says, "I believe that it will rain," one is giving a prediction based upon present weather conditions and knowledge of what has resulted from conditions like this in the past. But statements of the form "I believe in John" express evaluations rather than facts. Although one may base his judgment about John on the basis of John's past actions, this need not be so as when a child "believes in" or trusts his parent whether or not from an outside point of view the parent's past actions warrant that trust. Belief in God is similar for the man of faith wants to testify to his trust in God regardless of the factual situation.[17] It is claimed that such expressions of trust are analogous to expressions of trust in other persons so that the theological use of language can be interpreted as quite proper rather than as a misuse of language.

The Wittgensteinian philosopher of religion who justifies religious

16. The literature on this is vast. A few major representative statements are: P. H. Nowell-Smith, "Mr. Hare on Theology and Falsification," *Philosophical Quarterly*, 6 (July, 1956), 256–260; William H. Poteat, "God and the 'Private-I,'" reprinted in Dallas M. High, ed., *New Essays on Religious Language* (New York: Oxford University Press, 1969); H. H. Price "Belief 'In' and Belief 'That,'" *Religious Studies*, 1 (1964), 1–27; William Hordern, *Speaking of God* (London: The Epworth Press, 1965), pp. 132 ff.; Dallas M. High, *Language, Persons, and Belief* (New York: Oxford University Press, 1967), pp. 146ff.

17. Note that when some say "I believe in God" they really are saying "I believe that God exists" which may be a quite different expression. We have been taking "I believe in God" to mean an expression of trust.

language as a proper language game invites the charge that his whole program of defense limits the influence that religion can have in the secular world by his insistence that the meaning of religious utterances must be judged solely by the context of religion itself.[18] This limits religious meaning to its own context and, in realms outside, it will be quite meaningless. At the extreme, Ninian Smart argued that religious language must be judged by the particular context of each concrete religion and that there could be no single analysis of religious language since the contexts of various religions were so different.[19] While many theologians wanted to protect religious language from the criteria used to judge scientific language, they were unwilling to go so far in a defense that resulted in walling themselves into a compartment that was self-contained and of no relevance to the secular world.

To avoid this damaging thrust, some proponents of the Wittgensteinian apology denied that religious language was a separate language game and stressed instead its similarity to other games.[20] We have already noted this effort in the attempt to draw analogies between religious usage and ordinary usage in belief statements. Even though Wittgenstein did blur the lines between language games and did emphasize the resemblances among them, if there are such similarities between scientific and religious language uses then we are brought back to the question of why should we not, then, apply similar standards for linguistic meaning. In an effort to get away from the demands of testability made of scientific language, the Wittgensteinian apologist stressed the notion that meaning was determined by the context in which an expression occurred. This move insulated religious language from scientific language, but it also meant that theological pronouncements would be meaningless outside of religion. The latter predicament would prevent communications with nonbelievers. Frightened by this unexpected turn of events, apologists backed away from making language games exclusive of one another and claimed similarities among them. But if there are similarities, then perhaps similar criteria of meaning rather than different ones can be

18. Cf. Kai Nielsen, "Wittegensteinian Fideism," *Philosophy*, 42, no. 161 (July, 1967), 191–209.

19. Ninian Smart, *Reasons and Faiths* (London: Routledge & Kegan Paul, 1958).

20. Dallas High, *Language, Persons, and Belief*, pp. 81ff; D. Z. Phillips, "Religious Beliefs and Language-Games," *Ratio*, 12, no. 1 (June, 1970), 26–46.

employed. Here again, we see that part of the reluctance to allow a common set of criteria for meaning resulted from a misunderstanding of the nature of scientific language. Assuming that scientific language was unambiguous, precise, and easily falsifiable, philosophers of religion knowing that religious language was ambiguous, vague, and difficult to falsify, fell into the trap of building a defense so safe that they themselves could not escape from it unless they paradoxically retreated to similarities of expression without similarity of criteria for meaning.

Another response to the problem of justifiying religious language similar to that based upon the later Wittgenstein developed out of apologies based upon the work of J. L. Austin. Denying that meaning could only be associated with factual language, Austin developed the notion that language possessed a nonpropositional illocutionary force that conveyed a meaning by the act which speech performed rather than the object or event to which it referred.[21] Austin not only cited commands, but many other types of linguistic utterance like oaths of office or the "I do" of the marriage ceremony as examples of performatives. He then developed a typology for these forms of speech acts: (1) constatives that state, report, guess, warn, bet, and estimate; (2) commissives that promise, pledge, threaten, covenant, and undertake; (3) exercitives that order, decree, appoint, name, and give; (4) behabitives that thank, praise, apologize, blame, and confess; and (5) verdictives that judge, rate, find, grade, and value. By modifying these categories to suit theological usages, Donald Evans argued that religious language had meaning as performative language that expressed the self-involvement of the speaker.[22] This self-involvement was founded in depth experiences expressed in personal encounter, a numinous experience, moral responsibility, despair, and compassion. Taking the biblically based belief, "God is the Creator of the world," Evans attempted to demonstrate that it was a "behabitive-commissive and expressive utterance" and self-involving since creation should be viewed as a performative action including command, appointment, evaluation and pledge. In contrasting scientific and religious language, Evans found the former logically neutral (without self-

21. J. L. Austin, *How to Do Things with Words* (New York: Oxford University Press, 1965).
22. Donald D. Evans, *The Logic of Self-Involvement* (London: SCM Press, 1963).

involvement), comprehensible impersonally, and testable by observations. Religious language, he asserted possessed none of these qualities as it was self-involving, subjective, and untestable.[23] Here again, we find a strong declaration of the separation of scientific and religious language. The assumption that scientific language is testable by observation is far too strong. Most scientific statements are not testable by direct observation and one cannot build a strong logical relationship between unobservable theoretical statements and observation statements. We have also noted that observation statements are given form and character by theories, though it is possible that the theory-laden observation statements may be neutral with respect to this theory. Nor are scientific statements completely free from subjective factors. Theories are accepted partly upon the basis of sociological and historical factors as well as upon the basis of what empirical data exists. The reigning paradigm in science often determines the kinds of answers that will be acceptable to scientific questions. These beliefs of what will be acceptable influence the acceptance or rejection of both experimental data and theoretical speculations. To claim that the degree of subjectivity involved in scientific language, however, is just as great as that in religious language would be just as gross an exaggeration as the assertion that science escapes subjectivity completely.

The most extreme separation between scientific and religious language can be found among those theologians who assumed that religious discourse was uttered in a self-contained realm of meaning which required no justification. Both dialectical theologians in the tradition of Kierkegaard and many who emphasized the symbolic nature of religion exemplify this position. The early works of Karl Barth stressed the objective nature of theological language.[24] God was the subject who spoke the objective Word of God and the Church's dogmatic task was to

23. Donald D. Evans, "Difference Between Scientific and Religious Assertions," in *Science and Religion: New Perspectives on the Dialogue*, ed. Ian G. Barbour (New York: Harper & Row, 1968).

24. Karl Barth, *Church Dogmatics, The Doctrine of the Word of God*, Vol. 1, pt. 1 (Edinburgh: T. & T. Clark, 1955), pp. 1–30; see also his *The Epistle to the Romans*, tr. from the sixth edition by Edwyn C. Hoskyns (London: Oxford University Press, 1933). The prefaces to the various editions present a sketch of the development of Barth's thought.

test religious language by the standard of this objective Word disclosed in scripture as Jesus Christ. Barth thought that it was all right for the theologian to use the language of science or philosophy or any other discipline in his statements, just so long as the hearer did not begin to associate scientific or philosophical meanings with the words instead of the proper theological meanings derived from the revelation of the Word. Barth was painfully aware of this problem since he had used Kierkegaard's terminology in his earlier writings and had subsequently been accused of being an existentialist. Denying this vigorously, he purged the later editions of his famous *Church Dogmatics* of these terms.[25] This rejection of the criteria of science and philosophy as applicable to religious language stemmed from his belief that secular languages were the work of sinful man and, therefore, imperfect. Starting with an evaluation of man and the world also meant, according to Barth, that one was committed to a viewpoint that prohibited him from establishing the objectivity of God. For Barth, to begin with human criteria for truth and meaning was to limit the concept of God to one that was subjective.[26]

Interpreters of religion who emphasize its symbolic character assume an almost complete separation between scientific and religious languages for reasons quite different from those of Barth. They view religious language as a symbolic expression that guarantees its own meaning by virtue of the nature of the symbols themselves. According to this position, there are traditional symbols found in most religions about which man can center his existence. Mircea Eliade, the historian of religions, has identified a number of these archetypal symbols: the sacred tree, the cosmic center, sacred time, etc., and has argued that without some form of religious expression that recognizes these symbols, man will be unable

25. Ibid., *The Doctrine of the Word of God*, pp. 1–30.

26. The later Barth admitted that he was too stringent in excluding secular knowledge in his early period and was willing to allow secular knowledge about man that was in accord with theological anthropology. Cf. Karl Barth, *The Humanity of God* (Richmond: John Knox Press, 1960). Theologians after Barth have attempted to eliminate the distinction between subjective and objective by interpreting religious discourse as language events in which the Word discloses itself. Cf. Gerhard Ebeling, *Word and Faith* (London: SCM Press, 1963); Ernst Fuchs, *Studies of the Historical Jesus* (London: SCM Press, 1964); Heinrich Ott, "The Historical Jesus and the Ontology of History," in *The Historical Jesus and the Kerygmatic Christ*, ed. C. E. Braaten and R. A. Harrisville (Nashville: Abingdon Press, 1964).

to have a meaningful life.[27] The reality found in symbols is not to be judged by the standards of science or of any other discipline.

Paul Tillich also described religious language as a symbolic activity in which man participates in that which is symbolized.[28] He differentiated between signs and symbols by limiting the former to the act of "pointing to" whereas symbols not only "pointed" but also "participated in" the reality to which they pointed. Unlike Barth and Eliade, Tillich was unwilling to wall off a separate kingdom of symbols from the rest of the world. Instead, Tillich sought to relate numerous areas of human life to theology using depth psychology, literature, and history. To prevent symbols from standing alone, he insisted that there must be one nonsymbolic statement in religious language that could be understood literally.[29] Yet, Tillich's bridge from religious language to the secular world did not allow entrance into the realm of scientific language as he explicitly excluded science from the dimension of human existence with which religion dealt.[30] Not willing to allow religious language to be in a realm that is self-contained, Tillich was also not willing to allow it to be judged by the standards of meaning for scientific language.

Dialectical theologies and theologies based upon the intrinsic value of symbols both separate religious from scientific language. The consequences of this move are even more severe than those encountered by exponents of the Wittgensteinian defense of religious language. By assuming that the two realms of meaning are different, holders of these positions not only insure that criteria for scientific language cannot apply to religious discourse, but they also prevent religious claims from having any meaning in the scientific realm. The standards of truth for science are not applicable to religion, but neither are the standards of religion applicable to science. Believers are forced to live schizophrenic lives

27. Mircea Eliade, *The Sacred and the Profane* (New York: Harper Torchbooks, 1961); also his, *Images and Symbols* (London: Harvill Press, 1961).

28. Paul Tillich, "The Meaning and Justification of Religious Symbols," in *Religious Experience and Truth: A Symposium*, ed. Sidney Hook (Edinburgh: Oliver and Boyd, 1962); "Theology and Symbolism," in *Religious Symbolism*, ed. F. Ernest Johnston (New York: Harper, 1955); "The Religious Symbol," in *Symbolism in Religion and Literature*, ed. Rollo May (New York: George Braziller, 1960).

29. Paul Tillich, *Systematic Theology* (Chicago: University of Chicago Press, 1951), Vol. 1, pp. 264–265; Vol. 2 (1957), pp. 9–10.

30. Ibid., vol. 1, p. 21.

where what may be true of religion need not be true of science. Conflicts inevitably arise when both realms of discourse talk about the same problem, as when both speak about life and death or life after death. The religious man may seek refuge in a dialectic of time; when he is worshipping he adheres to the truths of religion, and when he lives in the world of science and technology he utilizes scientific truths. Communication from one realm to the other also becomes difficult for, if the symbolic realm of religion remains completely insulated, then people outside that realm will find it difficult to understand the meaning of the symbols especially since such meanings are determined exclusively by the context of the realm. Those who employ the family of resemblances for the Wittgensteinian language game approach do offer access to religious language, but, at the same time, they weaken their grounds for excluding criteria for the meaning of scientific language.

That the criteria for meaning for scientific language could apply to religious language was presumed by those who sought to eliminate its mythical and supernatural aspects. Believing that traditional religious language was incompatible with the findings of modern science, these interpreters sought to reduce religious discourse to language that was compatible. Rudolf Bultmann's program for demythologizing scripture was the most famous and influential effort in this direction.[31] Modern man, he argued, with his scientific outlook could no longer understand traditional religious language because biblical writers had assumed a mythological cosmology of a three-storied universe. Although contrary to our scientific outlook, if the theologian carefully unlocks the myths of scripture, he will find an understanding of human existence that does apply to the contemporary situation. Every questioner, however, speaks from a philosophical position whether he is willing to acknowledge it or not, and Bultmann believed that the proper philosophical stance from which to begin an analysis of religious language, especially scripture, was the existentialism of Heidegger. For him, the categories of the early Heidegger of *Being and Time* provide a meaningful description of the

---

31. Rudolf Bultmann, "New Testament and Mythology," in *Kerygma and Myth*, ed. Hans Werner Bartsch and tr. by Reginald H. Fuller, (London: SPCK, 1953) and Rudolf Bultmann, *Jesus Christ and Mythology* (New York: Charles Scribner's Sons, 1958). Note that Tillich explicitly engaged in limited programs of demythologizing scripture.

nature of "authentic" human existence. Having assumed the applicability of the standards of scientific language to the religious situation, Bultmann then retreated from that assumption when he located the *correct* (non-mythological) meaning of religion in the world of personal existence and not in the realm of science. Modern science exposes the fact that New Testament theology is mythological, but it can give little or no insight into the ultimate meaning of life. Bultmann was convinced that the existentialist interpretations of man resulting from demythologizing scripture were not themselves another form of mythology so that they were not subject to the criteria of scientific language. In fact, he talked of existentialist language as being "analogical" rather than "mythological."[32]

R. B. Braithwaite sought to reduce religious language to ethical language.[33] So much of it was contrary to empirical fact that one could not accept it in a literal sense. Yet one could still derive moral insights from the stories even though he knew them to be false. This was the case whenever we read literature, for though we knew a novel to be fictitious, we could still gain moral insights from it. Braithwaite acknowledged that ethical language was not directly verifiable, but he contended that it was compatible with empiricism because the intentions of the speaker of moral discourse could be tested against his actions. Since religious language was in reality ethical language clothed in fictitious stories, it too could qualify as meaningful.[34]

Braithwaite allowed the standard for the meaning of scientific language to apply not only to the mythical language of religion, but also to the view of religious language that he proposed. Bultmann had gone only half way in claiming that the criteria for meaning of scientific language applied to religious language for he retreated back into a separate realm of meaning when he offered an existentialist interpretation. Yet the criteria of a weakened version of verifiability that Braithwaite presented really does not deal with the problems of confirmation that scientists actually encounter. We have seen earlier that there remains a large number of unverifiable scientific statements after one has isolated those few that are

32. Cf. ch. 5 in *Jesus Christ and Mythology*.

33. R. B. Braithwaite, *An Empiricist's View of the Nature of Religious Belief* (Cambridge: Cambridge University Press, 1955).

34. Others made this claim. Cf. Ronald W. Hepburn, *Christianity and Paradox* (London: Watts, 1958), especially pp. 294–295.

testable by observation in the empirical world. Even a weakened principle of verification will not do as a criterion of meaning for scientific language.

Whatever the approach to religious language, two mistaken assumptions have been made about it. The first assumes that certain simple standards for meaning wrongly believed as applicable to scientific language can be used as the criteria for meaning in religious language. Thinking that scientific language could be verified or falsified, early positivists demanded that religious language be verifiable or falsifiable if it was to be considered meaningful. And those who protected religious language by positing a different realm of meaning were convinced that religious language was not testable. The second assumption consisted of treating religious language as if it were all of a single type. Critics who found no situation in which a statement like "God is love" could be falsified seemed to presume that such a statement was typical of all religious language and that its failure condemned all religious discourse to meaninglessness. No acknowledgement was made that there might be religious statements that were not expected to be falsifiable. Even defenders often fell into the same trap as did those who interpreted religious language almost exclusively as convictional "I-language." And these two assumptions were not unrelated, for it was the oversimplified demands for meaning that led to the oversimplified responses.

In believing that there should be similarities between scientific and religious language, early positivists were not wrong. Their mistake came from the employment of standards of meaning that could apply simply to neither scientific language nor religious language. Philosophers of religion, however, seemed unaware that the challenge made to religious language could prove equally disastrous if applied to scientific language.[35] Among philosophers of science, that scientific statements could not be easily falsified came as no surprise, and yet philosophers of religion recoiled in shock at the difficulty in demonstrating that religious statements were falsifiable.[36] There needs to be some evidential basis for

35. Dallas High suggested that the conception of scientific language by which religious language was indicted might well be misunderstood. Cf. his *Language, Persons, and Belief* (New York: Oxford University Press, 1967) p. 42.

36. J. Kellenberger proves the exception as he challenges the challenge of falsification in his "The Falsification Challenge," *Religious Studies*, 5, (1969) 69–76. This is re-reprinted in an appendix of his *Religious Discovery, Faith and Knowledge* (Englewood Cliffs: Prentice-Hall, 1972).

language if it is to qualify as genuine knowledge and this evidence cannot be protected by the dialectical assumption that religion occurs in a self-contained realm of meaning. For to allow the latter would be both to prevent communication of religious beliefs to nonbelievers and to prevent religion from having any relevance to the secular world. Religious language must be testable in the sense that common experiences must be available that are capable of interpretation in religious terms and symbols.[37] Unlike science, these common experiences need not all be observable since much of religious expression involves feelings and desires.

The language of religion is often divided into two basic categories similar to the theoretical-observation distinction found in descriptions of science.[38] The language of religion, like observation language, is said to be primary where "religion" is defined as a "human response to the divine." These statements are simply given and cannot be questioned as to their existence. Men do profess to have "seen God" or to have "felt Christ's presence in their lives," or "to have been absorbed into the Wholly Other" in a mystical trance. Collecting all of the utterances of religious men about their experiences of the divine yields the so-called primary "language of religion." The second type of language, akin to theoretical language, is "theological language." Derived from reflections upon the primary language of religion, theological language seeks to interpret or systematize "religion." Since theological language is inferred from religious experience, it cannot be directly verified in the way that a man who has had a vision or intuition "knows" that he has had it. Just as theoretical language in science was thought to differ from observation language, theology was distinguished from the language of religion in that the former was not accessible to experience. This distinction shows just which statements could be accepted as given and legitimate and which could be open to question. The statement, "I have had a vision of God," can be accepted if one trusts the man giving the testimony. But to infer from such a statement that God exists asserts a theological claim that may be disputed. One would question what the nature of the "God" of the vision was; was it an image or a blinding light or a vague

37. This point will be developed more fully in chapter 5.
38. Cf. John A. Hutchison, *Language and Faith* (Philadelphia: Westminster Press, 1963).

apparition? If this "God" is claimed to be the same "God" as the theologian talked about in statements asserting the "existence of God," then one would have to ask how the person possessing such experience knew it to be the same. If the owner of the vision claimed that the concept, "God," that he saw had been given to him by a theological tradition, then critics objected to a circularity in his argument. How could he possibly argue that the primary experience of God which he had in a vision could validly demonstrate the existence of God, when he had assumed the existence of the notion of God to begin with? Exactly this question arose in debates about Jesus. Theologians like Schweitzer assumed that the Jesus described in the New Testament was different from the Jesus which men professed to have experienced in faith.[39] Schweitzer distinguished between the "Jesus of History," which he believed to be hidden behind the motives and styles of the gospel writers, and the "Christ of faith." Bultmann did the same thing when he separated Jesus, the historical man, from the Jesus of the proclamation of the early Church. These divisions rest upon the assumption that the language of religion is different from the language of theology; theological statements were disputable, religious statements were the primary statements of religious faith.

The division between religious and theological language fails because those who profess to have a religious experience use theological terms to describe their experience. The religious tradition in which they live provides them with the terminology necessary to talk about their experience. Mystics in the Judaeo-Christian tradition speak of their mystical unions as encounters with "God" or with the "light of God" and by the term "God" they mean the same God that is found in scripture and worshipped in the church. On the way to union, mystics feel the smallness of themselves and describe this as the state of their own "sinfulness" in contrast to the goodness and majesty of God. If the mystic had been brought up in a different religious tradition, he would have used a different terminology to describe his moments of ecstasy. Hindus in the Advaita Vedanta tradition speak of the atman (soul or breath) becoming one with the Brahman, while Zen Buddhists participate in the harmony

39. Albert Schweitzer, *The Quest of the Historical Jesus* (New York: Macmillan, 1960), p. 3.

of nature and Muslim mystics profess a vision of Allah. Theological traditions provide the religious man with terms to interpret his experiences. Using these terms as descriptions of the divine presence, he is often not conscious that he is "interpreting" at all. The religious man claims to "see" God in his vision just as a scientist may claim to "see" subatomic particles when they are presented with a curved series of droplets in a cloud chamber. A theological tradition offers a way of looking at certain experiences; the particular tradition tells us what to look for and how to describe an experience when we possess it. The parallel with theoretical terms is striking, for in science theories both pose the question and also provide the researcher with the terminology and the context in which the question can be answered. There are, however, differences in that while theoretical language informs observations, theological language interprets experiences not all of which are open to public scrutiny. Statements of the mystic, for example, cannot be confirmed unless one has had a similar mystical experience.

Those who object to this fusion of theological and religious language often do so on grounds that such a combination produces a circularity fatal to religion. They ask, how is it possible for one to offer religious experiences as evidence for the existence of God when the term "God" has already been presupposed by the one claiming to have had such an experience? This objection is similar to that made against the theory-laden character of observation statements. It was claimed that the breakdown of the theoretical-observation distinction leads to a loss of objectivity, since allowing theoretical terms to affect the character of "what" is observed means that one observes what one wants to find rather than "hard facts." These objections fail for critics of both scientific and religious language assume that the model of explanation for each is based upon logical deduction. They want premises that are established by inference from the empirical world independent of the conclusion, so that the argument can be considered to be conclusive. Like scientific explanations, theologies are conceptual patterns of knowledge in which there are empirical, experiential, and imaginative elements all woven together.

Earlier, we saw that although all observation statements are theory-laden, some may be loaded by theories other than the one for which the investigator may be seeking an empirical test. Whether a statement is classified as an observation or a theoretical statement also depends upon the context in which it is employed. Relative to one theory it may be a neutral observation statement while in relation to another, it may be theoretical. By analogy, one should find expressions of religious experience that are neutral relative to one theology even though derived from another. Unfortunately, this analogy does not seem to hold, for while there are numerous scientific theories that are different and yet complement one another, usually theologies are accepted or rejected as alternatives and one does not find this theology applying to this kind of experience and that theology applying to that kind of experience. This lack of analogy does not mean that theologies have no empirical evidence, but that the overall outlook with which they interpret that evidence cannot be tested even with partial independence from the context in which it occurs. Simply stated, science does possess more objective testability than religion, but one should, at his peril, argue that science is *completely* objective and religion completely subjective.[40]

Critics of religious language have usually upheld ordinary language as the paragon of neutral observation language that should be used in testing religious discourse. Why not use simple descriptive terms applicable to everyday objects like chairs and tables as terms descriptive of religious experience? Would not this provide us with a neutral language that was free from theory and theology? And if religious utterances cannot generate statements expressible in ordinary terms, then discard such theology as nonsense. Would not ordinary language provide us with a neutral language that is free from theory and theology? Unfortunately not, for simple common sense language is based upon a theoretical description of the world (naive realism) that often turns out to be false relative to a particular theory. Science often demonstrates that widely accepted physical laws are contrary to our normal perceptions and intuitions. That length, time, and mass are all relative to velocity and not absolute shocks us when we first encounter such notions, because we have been used to dealing with fixed bodies and standard intervals of time. And the language of common sense is not adequate for religion either. Religious experiences cannot be described as if they were

40. This point will also be developed more fully in chapter 5.

common objects; one of the major qualities of such an experience is that it differs from ordinary life and must be expressed in theological terms. Without theological terminology, religious experience would be blind and unintelligible.

There is one "language of religion" which as a category includes both religious and theological language. The attempt to separate religious and theological language fails; statements describing religious experience are theology-laden. Although this distinction will not hold up, it does make sense to talk about the various uses of religious language.[41] Mystics are not trying to reflect upon their own experience when they try to express their feelings even though they borrow theological language to do so. Theologians are *reflecting* upon experiences rather than expressing their feelings even though they use the data of religion as the basis for their work. Thus, if one talks about the "language of religious experience," he does not mean that this is an exclusive domain which does not use theological terminology, but, rather, that language in the hands of the worshipper or mystic is being used in a certain way. Nor is theological language different from religious language, but to speak of theological language means to describe the language used in formulating an explanation. The languages are fluid and used interchangeably, but the functions are different.

Debates about whether religious language can be defended philosophically have tended to consider religious utterances as if they were of one type, empirically testable, or ethical, or mythical, or metaphoric, or convictional. Yet the man of faith and the theologian rarely express their beliefs in religious language of a single type. Usually, statements of religious beliefs include expressions of conviction and tradition stating historical facts, personal feelings, and often ethical admonitions. Metaphors abound in such language and the critic, forgetting that scientific language also uses metaphor, indicts religious discourse as ambiguous and metaphoric. To express his beliefs, the religious man draws upon tradition as found in scripture, in the statements of

41. Cf. Dallas High, *Language, Persons, and Belief* (New York: Oxford University Press, 1967). High argued convincingly that one ought to speak of the "religious uses of language" rather than "religious language." Richard N. Bell makes a similar claim rejecting the terms "religious language" in his "Wittgenstein and Descriptive Theology," *Religious Studies*, 5, (1969) 1–18.

religious experience of earlier believers, and in the church's theology. We shall examine briefly each of these sources in order to present a more comprehensive picture of religious language.

All religions seem to have a body of sacred literature that has a hallowed status and which influences the entire language of that religion. Theological utterances as well as statements of personal conviction and experience are filled with scriptural language. One would like to say that scripture contains the tradition of a religion, but that would be incorrect for tradition is also to be found in creeds, in the personal accounts of saints, and in ecclesiastical history. Nor is scripture only a record of the religious experiences of the founders of the religion for it contains many other types of literature: a moral code, ritual procedures, etc. Scripture occupies a peculiar position as religious language, for it usually possesses a special status. Often it is claimed that all religious discourse must be scriptural in character in order to be legitimate. Hindus want all of their later works to be Vedic, just as Christians want their pronouncements to be biblical and Muslims want their theology to be in accord with the Koran. There seems to be almost universal agreement among followers of a religion that sacred literature cannot be eliminated and that it must have some integral role to play in the life of the religion if only as part of the tradition rather than as the sole source of authority.

One of the major types of literary expression found in scripture is historical narrative. The history of the Israelites tells of a people that spread from Ur of the Chaldees into Israel and then wandered into Egypt only to return to Israel, there to form a short-lived kingdom that was overrun by the Chaldeans, the Babylonians, and finally the Romans. In this legendary narrative, we read of the heroic acts of great leaders who urged a recalcitrant group of wanderers on to warfare and to faithfulness to Yahweh. That the events behind these legends are real is well attested by other literature and by present day archaeology.

Another major narrative is the life of Jesus. The historical man, Jesus, did live and walk about Palestine; he attracted disciples through his preaching and he was killed by the Romans. The various accounts of Jesus in the gospels are like the story of the Israelites, filled with embellishments and written with definite theological purposes in mind. And though it is extremely difficult to differentiate between what Jesus may have actually said and what was added by the writers, it would be a mistake to claim that there is nothing in the narratives about the life of Jesus, for most embellishments are based upon real events.

Myths are among the most notorious forms of literature present in scripture. Since myth was so widely misunderstood as a completely fictional account, many believers firmly resisted this label as applicable to the stories which they loved. But myth, understood as an imaginative and speculative explanation of how the world came to be, can offer an interpretation that yields insights into the beliefs of the writers. The two accounts of God's creation in Genesis bear witness to the beliefs of the writers that it was Yahweh who was fully responsible for the formation of the world. The fact that these myths are similar to others like the Enuma Elish of Babylon does not undermine the message that is conveyed, but helps us in our understanding of the literary structure and of the ways of conceiving the world which ancient men possessed. Interpreters of myth run into difficulty when they either try to take it literally or when they seek to dismiss the myth as nonsense. Myths are conceptual patterns filled with metaphors, and as such, are highly suggestive. They speculate about how the world might have been created; through repetition, early man came to accept them as actual descriptions of what happened in fact, rather than as imaginative speculations of the author. Only when myth is contrasted with another view of reality do men remember again that this was a speculative account and not a literal one. Myths, then, are unlocked; their structure is examined as a hypothetical device and insights are gleaned from how other men in other times looked at the world and the divine.

We have already noted that sacred literature abounds in poetry and detailed descriptions of rituals. Poetry expresses the emotions of joy, sorrow, praise, love, and a host of other human feelings. Some of it is explicitly theological calling upon God for intervention, while some of it seems distinctly secular as in some of the love poetry. Anyone who has read Deuteronomy or the Vedas has been both fascinated and bored by the endless details of how to perform rituals properly. In all of these literary forms, metaphors abound. The language is rich in its literary expression and the words are usually successful in conveying the passionate feelings of those who participated in these rites.

Elsewhere in the Bible, explicit metaphors occur and many times form dominant themes as in expressions like "God is love," or "I am the way, the truth, and the light." These metaphors suggest hypothetical meanings for the terms "God" or "Jesus." By continued use in the church, however, they have become shopworn and trite. No longer do they suggest the mysterious nature of God and shock the hearer. Nor does modern man bring to these metaphors the same assumptions about the nature of the world as did ancient man for whom these expressions were meaningful and vibrant.

Most scriptures also contain ethical exhortations prescribing a way of life for the believers. These may be attached to rituals as prerequisites whose performance is necessary so that the ceremony may succeed, or they may be commands of God received through the mouths of prophets telling the faithful how to act.

This brief description of scriptural language could be extended almost indefinitely to include parables, proverbs, miracle stories, wisdom literature, etc. Extremely varied, scriptural language is difficult to classify into any one type. To those who claim that it is all poetry and metaphor, one can respond by producing historical narrative; to those who claim that it is a literal history of Israel and later of Jesus, one has only to bring forth a few myths to contradict that notion. The interesting point about scripture and its relation to the language of religion is that rarely is all of it ever used or accepted in a theological explanation. In formulating a theological account, some elements of scripture are selected as relevant and others are ignored with selection dependent upon the religious experience and the theological tradition (in addition to scripture) of the believer. These two sources, religious experience and theological tradition, generate the questions that men bring to scripture. Neither of them is mutually exclusive nor are they themselves uninfluenced by scriptural language. But, they are surely different from scripture and provide language of their own that a believer uses when he formulates his own religious views.

The language of religious experience ranges from the very subjective and metaphoric language of the mystic to the more common experience of God's revelation professed by large numbers of committed believers. The mystic finds it difficult to communicate his experience to anyone else except, perhaps, other mystics. After the trance, he may describe it in theological or scriptural terms as a union with "God" or a union with the "love of Jesus," but when he tries to say more than that he resorts to terms like the "ineffable" or the "sublime" or the "most beautiful and exhilirating experience" of his life. Or he may use a series of negatives to describe his experience: "It was like nothing in this world, it transcended all perceptions and thoughts, my self was completely obliterated." The mystic may find himself so inspired that he uses poetry to describe what has happened to him as Indian mystics did in the later Upanishads. The language that the mystic employs usually does convey the deep and rich feelings of ecstasy, and sometimes the despair, that he has experienced.

The language of religious experience tends to be less colorful and more positive than that used by mystics. Groups using this language are larger than circles of mystics, but they have the same problem of communicating their truths to those outside the fold. Instead of claiming a direct union with the divine, those professing to have religious experience say that they "feel the presence of God in their lives" or that they can "intuit the love and grace of God redeeming them." Such feelings and intuitions lead them to believe that God has, indeed, revealed himself to them both in scripture and in their hearts.

Groups that profess religious experience also tend to exhibit public factors as well as private experiences to support their theological claims. Unlike the mystic, who relies solely upon his subjective experience to confirm his beliefs, those who claim some form of revelation offer events in history as well as the feelings of God's presence to support their claims. They assert that God has acted in history and, although unbelievers may question the interpretation of these events, the fact that the events themselves did occur cannot be disputed. The Israelites, for example, did flee from Egypt to Israel whether or not one agrees that God helped them. Or events in the life of Jesus are interpreted and expanded by the personal testimonies of those who have felt their "hearts strangely warmed." By expanding the evidence for theological claims from the purely subjective of the mystic to interpretations of historical events, those professing shared religious experiences allow their theological propositions to become publicly debatable. But the discussion is still limited in its scope, for possession of religious experience is used as a guarantee for the veracity of the interpretation of historical events, and nonbelievers without such experiences find such interpretations immune to criticism.

Theology offers the third source of religious language. This includes the work of systematic theology, historical theology, biblical theology, and apologetic theology. We have already seen that there remains no clearcut division between theological and religious language, but the two have a difference in function; the theologian *reflects* upon experience while the religious man *expresses* it. Even these functions, however, may intermingle as theologians possess their own religious experiences which are bound to influence their judgments.

Although many believers are influenced by systematic and philosophical theologians, the most pervasive theological influence comes from creeds. When the Christian repeatedly utters the opening lines of the Apostle's Creed—"I believe in God the Father almighty, maker of heaven and earth. . . "—he fixes in his mind certain associations that may be used to describe and interpret his own religious feelings. The metaphoric association of God with the function of a cosmic father finds the reinforcement in the Nicene Creed as part of the Trinity. The image of God as a creator father forms one of the major concepts of Christian theology and both personal experiences and the events of scripture are interpreted in light of it. That Jesus is of one substance with God, the father, and that he is not only fully divine but also fully human, one person with two natures, was established by the Nicene Creed and the Chalcedonian formula and these doctrines have been affirmed over and over again down through the centuries. Creeds result from the church's desire to establish certain beliefs by concensus and while they are subject to the limitations of decisions arrived at by political methods, their influence upon subsequent generations is tremendous as they provide the very concepts used to express and reflect upon religious experience.

Scripture, the language of religious experience, and theology are all sources for religious language. Since the body of scripture is fixed, its language is independent of the other two. Interpretations of scripture, however, do depend upon religious experience and theology. Neither theology nor the language of religious experience can be understood as exclusive of each other; the language of each enterprise borrows heavily from the other. When the religious man sets forth his beliefs, he usually borrows language from all three sources. Wherever possible, he borrows images and concepts from both scripture and theology to describe his own feelings and intuitions, and his own statements of conviction are often borrowed from creeds or other forms of theology. He may claim that he knows these to be true because he has had the experience of God, the father, the same god who appears in the Old and New Testaments. He may view certain events in the life of the Israelites and Jesus as actual historical fact and others as mythology developed by the writers to testify to their beliefs. His reasons for these judgments may be based upon methods of literary criticism and his presuppositions about why scripture was written. When his experience of faith is challenged, he may reply that while rational reasons cannot be given for it, he knows that it is true because he has surely experienced it. Or he may claim that his faith centers in God as a symbol for the "ultimate" in the world.

Drawing their concepts from scripture, the traditions of religious experience, and theology, believers set forth their notions of religion in a conceptual pattern that unified various aspects of experience, historical data, belief, and theological tradition. The pattern is a unity in that the various segments are put together into a coherent whole. There may be paradoxes within as well as gaps of interpretation and unanswered questions, but for the believer it is the pattern of explanation and insight that he has adopted for his religious dimension of life. The language of the pattern varies, including poetry, myth, ethical commands, historical narrative, and convictional statements. Much of this language, but not all of it, is metaphorical as the believer seeks to express a divine reality that extends beyond the normal range of experience. Although the conceptual pattern which a believer will present to express his beliefs is filled with metaphoric and esoteric language, these are embedded in ordinary language that is available to all. If this were not so, critics would not be able to discuss religious issues. Those who are critical may throw up their hands in horror when a believer produces the evidence of personal experience to justify segments of the pattern, but they know what the defender means by such language even though they deny its validity.

The meaningfulness of religious language cannot be assessed by considering individual statements and determining whether they are testable.

Such procedures, widely employed in debates about religious language, fail to comprehend the nature of religious discourse as a complex language composed of many different types of expression and bound together in a theological pattern. Only a very few statements will be testable and these will be expressed in theological and scriptural jargon making it even more difficult to find testable statements that are neutral relative to the theology in which they occur. Much of religious language can be acknowledged as metaphoric and imprecise, but those qualities may be of advantage rather than indications of failure for as the theologian seeks to speculate about what is difficult to express, he resorts to highly speculative and suggestive language. After we have seen that scientists need to employ the same kind of speculative device, the metaphor, it is difficult to condemn religious men for the same linguistic usage. We must explore, however, the nature of metaphor and assess carefully the kinds of metaphors used by scientists and theologians before drawing some conclusions that would be too hasty at this point.

III

The language of metaphor

For some time it has been seriously doubted that metaphor could be a legitimate device for the expression of genuine knowledge. Many philosophers believed that when arguments were weak, metaphor was invoked to serve as a distraction from obvious faults. It has been viewed as more expressive of emotive feelings than of cognitive information. Metaphor was acceptable in poetry and literature for there the purpose of the writer was to convey intense feelings about the nature of human existence. But when metaphor appeared in science or philosophy, efforts were immediately undertaken to eliminate it, for it was considered to be dangerous rather than beneficial. This attitude was part of the reason that philosophers objected to religious language, which was notorious in its use of metaphor. Religious language was thought to be emotive, not only because it could not be directly and publicly verified or falsified, but also because it employed metaphors. When positivists found that scientists also utilized such infamous linguistic devices, they strove to eliminate them by representing scientific language in formal logic. Without metaphor, however, scientists could not change the meanings of terms and suggest new hypotheses. That scientific terms necessarily change their meanings seriously undermined the view that scientific language could be unambiguous and precise.

The discovery that science needs metaphor does not by itself guarantee the legitimacy of the religious use of metaphor. It merely eliminates a negative argument; to object to religion solely because it uses metaphor is not a sufficient argument for the same criticism could be leveled at science. Nor does the scientific use of metaphor guarantee that metaphor is always a proper tool for the expression of knowledge. Some poetical metaphors may well express emotions rather than concepts. What we need is a theory that will differentiate among different uses of metaphor showing us which ones constitute knowledge claims and which ones seek to reveal deep human feelings and how these different functions are achieved. The development of a "tension theory" of metaphor by both philosophers and literary critics seeks to do just that—to offer an interpretation of the various forms and uses of metaphor.[1] During the last decade philosophers have moved far beyond Aristotle's notion of metaphor as the use of one word to stand for another. They want to show just how it is possible for some metaphors to create meaning, for others to express analogies, and for still others to become "dead" as they enter our everyday usage, and it is to this theory that we must attend if we are to understand the similarities and differences of the scientific and religious uses of metaphor.

The essence of a tension theory is that if a metaphor is taken literally, it produces absurdity. When we first hear the metaphor or see it in writing we are genuinely shocked by it. The new word or the juxtaposition of old terms is quite unnatural and produces an emotional response in us. When it was found that "particles" which were thought to be irreducible atoms could be divided as in the case of the nucleus, scientists were surprised and the word "particle" took on a new and metaphorical meaning. Or talking about "particles" that travel faster than the speed of light is similarly shocking. When the early Christians claimed that "God" has become man in Jesus, the Jews who heard this were stunned because their notion of Yahweh assumed that God was completely different from man. To say that God is light does not claim that "God" is the physical phenomenon of photons. Even commonplace metaphors like "time flies" or to "see the point of a story" or to "hear from someone" when one received a letter all seem odd and strange when they are first used. Time does not literally "fly" in the sense that a bird does, nor do we literally "see" the point of a story in the sense of visual perception, nor do we

1. Cf. Earl R. MacCormac, "Metaphor Revisited," *The Journal of Aesthetics and Art Criticism*, 30 (Winter, 1971), 239–250; and "Metaphor and Literature," *The Journal of Aesthetic Education*, 6, no. 3 (July, 1972), 57–70. In these two essays and here in this chapter I draw upon standard sources for a tension theory of metaphor including: Douglas Berggren, "The Use and Abuse of Metaphor: I and II," *The Review of Metaphysics*, 16 (Dec., 1962), 237–258, and (March, 1963), 450–472; Max Black, *Models and Metaphors: Studies in Language and Philosophy* (Ithaca: Cornell University Press, 1962); Northrop Frye, *Anatomy of Criticism: Four Essays* (Princeton: Princeton University Press, 1957); Colin Turbayne, *The Myth of Metaphor* (New Haven: Yale University Press, 1962); and Philip Wheelwright, *Metaphor and Reality* (Bloomington: Indiana University Press, 1962).

"hear" in the auditory sense when we receive a letter. Tension is the emotional shock produced in the hearer by an intentional misuse of language. We are not comfortable seeing ordinary language used in this fashion and in the sense of surprising us and causing us to pause and consider what is meant by this strange juxtaposition of words, metaphors when they are new are the occasions for emotional responses.

All metaphors that produce legitimate tension consist of two referents. Often it is said that these two parts are the well-known and the less-well-known. The well-known has been called the "tenor" or underlying idea (principle subject) and the less-well-known the "vehicle" or imagined nature.[2] This certainly fits the case of "particle" where the principle idea was that of solid irreducible atoms (tenor) and the imagined hypothesis was that these objects could be subdivided (vehicle). Yet these categories are not precise for not only does the old sense of particle take on a new meaning, but the new meaning of subatomic physics where "particles" do divide also retains many of the properties of the older notion of "particle" such as solidity. There is an interaction in all metaphors between the two referents.[3] Consider the metaphor "Man is a wolf." Here "man" takes on the qualities of wolf-like behavior such as grouping together in bands and preying on his fellow man in a rapacious manner. But "wolf" may also take on the characteristics of human behavior so that when we see wolves in zoos or in the wilderness, we think of them as possessing certain human qualities. When it was claimed that God was man in Jesus, certainly both the notion of God was altered as well as the notion of man. The advent of this metaphor led to the doctrine of the Trinity and to many theological doctrines of man that include the possibility of man participating in divinity through his own humanity. To say that "God is man" alters both our notion of God and our notion of man.

At this point we should note that when we describe a metaphor as possessing two referents, we do not necessarily mean that it is composed of two "words." The word "particle," for example, could be a metaphor in quantum mechanics because it referred both to its Newtonian use as a

2. I. A. Richards, *The Philosophy of Rhetoric* (New York: Oxford University Press, 1936).

3. Max Black, "Metaphor," in *Metaphors and Models* (Ithaca: Cornell University Press, 1962).

solid irreducible atom *and* to its new properties of divisibility and trans-mutation into energy. In other metaphors, such as "God is man" or "Man is a wolf," the two referents are explicit and consist of the juxtaposition of words not normally put together when they are first expressed. Our notion of metaphor as composed of two referents producing absurdity in the hearer extends to all grammatical forms including simile, synecdoche, metonymy, and catachresis just to name a few. We reject the old division between simile and metaphor on the grounds that both grammatical forms involve a comparison of the properties of both refer-ents. To say that "Man is like a wolf" and "Man is a wolf" are different is only to claim that the first simile explicitly *asks* the listener to compare the two while the latter does the same thing implicitly. When one hears "Man is a wolf," he must consider the ways in which it might be possible for men to be *like* wolves and wolves to be *like* men. Simile as a grammatical form explicitly reminds us to compare the two referents. And if the juxtaposi-tion of referents in a metaphor rested upon no likeness at all, then the metaphor would not just be strange, it would be unintelligible. There would be no way in which we could recognize one part as even possibly related to the other part.

Since taking metaphors literally produces absurdity and emotional shock, we must consider the metaphor "as if" it were true. Man is not a wolf and yet we consider what it would be like to be a wolf or for a wolf to be a man. This is what gives metaphor its hypothetical character; it is suggestive of new possibilities for meaning. The act of creating a new metaphor is the process of forming an imaginative hypothesis. Poets suggest new says of viewing the world or of considering human feel-ings by their novel use of language. Some of the ideas they propose seem plausible to us while others seem foreign and remote. Some of their suggestions express the ways in which we feel and others do not. When the author of Psalm 23 wrote: "The Lord is my shepherd . . ." the suggestion that God protected his people like a shepherd who guards his sheep had deep meaning for those believing that God had delivered them from adversity. But for those like Job who had been afflicted and tormented, the suggestion of God as a shepherd was so irrelevant as almost to be offensive. Scientists also make suggestions some of which find confirmation, as in seventeenth century mechanics where it was proposed that action could take place at a distance. To Aristotelians the notion that movement could take place without a force or impetus in direct contact with the object moved was absurd. Yet this metaphorical suggestion came to be expressive of what later scientists actually believed to be the case in nature. Bodies could be in motion without an impressed force. Yet other suggestions also expressed in metaphors never did become expressive of confirmed experience. We have already seen that the "funiculus" as an explanation of why mercury rose to a height of 29.5 inches was discarded. The history of science is filled with metaphorical terms that have since been discarded. We are familiar with the overthrow of the phlogiston theory and the refutation of ether.[4] There is nothing to stop us from *considering* that there is an invisible substance ether that is necessary for the propagation of light waves except scientific experiments that produce contrary evidence. There are still other scientific metaphors like the tachyon (a particle that travels faster than the speed of light) that remain speculative hypotheses; they are suggestions neither confirmed nor disconfirmed.[5]

Interestingly, the "as if" quality of many metaphors disappears altogether after a time. What may start out as a suggestive juxtaposition of referents filled with tension ends up as a commonplace part of our ordinary language. We call these dead or faded metaphors. When we say that "time flies" no one is shocked or surprised and we all know what we mean by this. Yet when the metaphor was first uttered, it did occasion surprise, for time is not literally something that flies. But it is expressive of how we do feel about time. Often our experience is that time passes swiftly like the swift flight of a bird. Certainly there are other occasions when "time drags" to use another metaphor. However, when we want to express our feelings of the rapid passage of time, we say "time flies." This metaphor was so expressive of human feelings that it was used over and over again. What started out as a misuse of language, the juxtaposition of "time" with the verb "fly," becomes a proper use. Gradually, through the repeated use of the metaphor, "fly" takes on the connotation of "rapid

4. James Bryant Conant, *The Overflow of the Phlogiston Theory* (Cambridge: Harvard University Press, 1950).

5. Roger G. Newton, "Particles That Travel Faster Than Light?" *Science*, 167, no. 3925 (March 20, 1970), 1569–74.

passage" in addition to that of "physical movement through the air." Just when this transition takes place is difficult to ascertain, but a glance at dictionaries of different periods clearly shows that words do change their meanings. To cite one example, consider the word "chaff." In Samuel Johnson's famous dictionary of 1755 this word meant the "refuse left after the process of threshing grain" and also "any worthless thing."[6] Undoubtedly, this began with a meaning associated with the winnowing of grain and then was extended to anything, like the husks or stalks, that was worthless in comparison to the grain itself. By 1966, dictionaries included another lexical entry for this word: "thin metallic strips that are dropped from an aircraft to create confusing signals on radarscopes."[7] This sense of the word is anything but worthless, especially if you are flying in an airplane and your life is dependent upon the success of the "chaff" in preventing your being intercepted or shot down. How could a word that had the meaning of "any worthless thing" come to have a technological and military meaning of something that was quite "worthwhile" and necessary? The change came, of course, through its use as a metaphor. Early in the development of antiradar devices, strips of metal were dropped from airplanes and found to have the effect of confusing the radar by causing many blips on the screen in addition to that of the airplane itself. The pieces of metal first used were the scraps from the milling process. This metal literally was "chaff." In addition, when the scrap metal was dropped from planes, it scattered and floated down much like straw would if it had been dropped in a similar fashion. Thus, the word "chaff" was chosen to describe the objects used to confuse radar because the metal chosen was scrap and useless relative to the manufacturing process and because the visual picture was similar to that of straw floating in the wind. "Chaff" was used as a metaphor—a well-known word was chosen to express a new meaning. "Worthless" material is considered *as if* it is "worthwhile." The latter usage is confirmed by its effect upon enemy radar and the "as if" quality disappears. This results in an added lexical entry in dictionaries.

6. Samuel Johnson, *A Dictionary of the English Language* (London: N. Strahan, 1755), reprinted by AMS Press, Inc., New York, 1967.
7. Jess Stein, ed., *Random House Dictionary of the English Language* (New York: Random House, 1966).

This is how a word like "particle" can move from a meaning that includes the properties of solidity and irreducibility to a meaning that includes divisibility and existence as a field of energy. The word still retains its concept of a definite entity as did the older concept so that "particle" in quantum mechanics is not completely different from the classical notion. Electrons and other subatomic particles are different from Newton's corpuscles in that they are not bits of matter and yet they are also still like them in that we can talk about them as single entities. We say that there are a discrete number of electrons orbiting the nucleus or that electrons jump from one energy level to another. Tension disappears in the metaphor as the "as if" quality is eliminated by the confirmation of the hypothesis.

In theology the concept of God has often had the status of a metaphor suggesting an hypothesis that is later widely accepted with the concurrent loss of tension. Since the reformation, Protestants have considered God as an absolute, transcendent being, invisible, immutable, all powerful and beneficent. Proposals by process theologians that God should be thought of as di-polar with one aspect absolute and another aspect relative and changing cause shock among those committed to the older meaning of the term.[8] The new metaphorical suggestion has a tension that the older one has lost. Whether the suggestion will be adopted and the metaphor pass into ordinary theological usage will depend upon the confirmation that this hypothesis does or does not receive in the minds of believers. Without such acceptance, the metaphor of God as a di-polar being will remain only a suggestive hypothesis. Reinterpretations of theological terms resulting in the formation of new theological metaphors have occurred over and over again. Dogmatic theologians who claim that theology is relatively unchanging have only to look at the entries for "God" in an etymological dictionary to find the contrary. "God" has had "tribal," "legal," "metaphysical" and "psychological" characteristics.

Tension in metaphors can be produced either by odd combinations of words or by actual contradictions in usage. When we say that we "see the point of a story," we do not actually "see" in a visual sense, and when this metaphor was first presented, the language seemed odd to the audience.

8. Cf. Charles Hartshorne, *The Divine Relativity* (New Haven: Yale University Press, 1964).

Until "seeing" came to mean "comprehending" or "understanding," to apply the notion of "seeing" to "the point of a story" was to misuse language, in that "seeing" was applicable to physical events rather than to themes in literature. This odd combination of words was startling because of our unfamiliarity with such a usage. Yet, such an oddity suggested a new way of considering literature, that of looking at the message as if it were a statement or an image. This was analogous to what interpreters of stories actually do in reducing the theme to a single statement when they comprehend a story, and so the metaphor, "to see the point of a story," became commonplace. Not only was our way of looking at a story changed, but the meaning of the verb "to see" took on the additional notion of "to comprehend." With familiarity came the loss of tensions and the simultaneous fading of the metaphor as it became a part of ordinary language.

Contradictions also produce tension when the parts of a metaphor are logically opposed to one another. Such opposition arose when the word "particle," which had been used to refer to solid irreducible particles, was employed to indicate entities that were divisible. Our commitment to the law of noncontradiction as a major feature of rationality leads us into a state of shock when we confront the simultaneous affirmation and negation of a common property found in a single term.

To consider the variance of meaning in metaphoric terms, it is necessary to distinguish between those properties which are analogous to the old meaning of the term and those properties which are suggestive in the context of the new metaphoric usage. Consider a term Q with properties $P_1, \ldots, P_n$ in a context C, that now appears as a metaphor Q' with properties $P_1', \ldots, P_n'$ in a new context C'. The tension of the metaphor Q' is produced by either of two cases. (Case 1): The P's that are replaced by P''s do not yield a logical contradiction, but are absurd in the sense that they result from category mistakes. Language is misused, but inconsistency cannot be demonstrated. (Case 2): The P''s that replace the P's do produce contradictions. But showing a contradiction between a P and a P' can be exceedingly difficult for the contexts C and C' in which they both appear are different. What may at first seem to be a contradiction may upon reflection not be demonstrable, since the different contexts generate terms with different meanings rather than a pair of contradictories. An example can be found in the use of "angular momentum" by Bohr in his atomic theory. These terms were employed by Bohr in their classicial sense even though the quantities that they designated were considered to be quantized rather than continuous. At first it looked as if there was a case of contradiction arising from the two uses of angular momentum. If angular mometum means the same thing in both theories, then we can have the contradictory pair of statements: "Angular momentum expresses a continuous function" and "Angular momentum expresses a discontinuous or quantized function." But scientists soon realized that they were dealing with two different phenomena, that of solid objects in classical mechanics and that of atomic particles in quantum mechanics. Then it was realized that "angular momentum" could have two different meanings when applied to the two different phenomena, thus destroying the contradiction. This has already been shown in the case of the metaphoric extension of "chaff" from a word meaning any worthless thing to a word expressing something quite worthwhile in the case of metallic chaff used to disrupt radar signals.

There are, however, many metaphors that do produce their tension by means of contradiction. Even though "particle" in classical mechanics possesses solidity and we know "particles" to be divisible in contemporary physics, it is difficult to describe the latter without conceiving of the traditional properties of particles. We are uneasy about modern particles that can be subdivided because such a conception contradicts our more usual notion that particles are the smallest units. And we do use "particle" ambiguously; sometimes we mean an irreducible particle and other times we mean a particle that can be divided as in subatomic physics.

Since all metaphors possess two referents and this juxtaposition produces an absurdity either by oddness or by outright contradiction, they rest upon an ambiguity of reading. The words can be read in their ordinary common traditional meaning or in their new and more suggestive absurd sense. Although all metaphors rest upon ambiguity for their very nature, not all ambiguous forms of language are metaphors. Many ambiguities of language are not metaphoric in that they do not surprise us with a novel way of considering things. We may be puzzled by a word usage as to exactly what it means, but such puzzlement does not necessarily produce tension in us either by outright contradiction or by oddity in our use of the language. For example, consider the sentence: "John took the leaves." Unless we know the context in which such a statement was uttered, we do not know whether the meaning is: (1) John picked up the leaves that had fallen from the tree; or, (2) John took several leaves from active service; or, (3) John took the leaves of a manuscript; or, (4) John took the leaves of the table. All of these usages are quite normal and none of them are a startling and fresh use of language characteristic of a metaphor. When the metaphor "Man is a wolf" was first used, it was ambiguous as to exactly how man was like a wolf for the literal equation of the two nouns was impossible. The absurdity of this ambiguous combination produced tension in the first hearers, and only after the analogy between the behavior of humans and the behavior of wolves was realized did the metaphor lose much of its tension and become commonplace.

Since we have seen that there is a process by which some metaphors are accepted as expressive of human knowledge and experience and thereby become a part of ordinary discourse, it can be asked whether all language is not, therefore, metaphorical. Could it not be argued that, because ordinary language is composed of so many successful metaphors, there is no way to judge the difference between ordinary language and metaphorical language, which we have insisted began with a misuse or odd use of the former? Although it is difficult to determine just when a metaphor ceases to be a live and tension-filled device and passes over into ordinary discourse, there is a distinction between the language which we use in everyday conversations and language which is hypothetical and speculative. Ordinary language does not surprise us. Even former metaphors that are now widely accepted do not cause us to pause and consider how it is possible to utter them. Ordinary discourse is expressive of commonplace experience; it is well confirmed and well established. We know what we mean when we speak, or at least think we do, whereas when live metaphors enter the conversation we feel uneasy about them as we are not sure that the usage does in fact express our feelings or our knowledge. One difference, then, between ordinary discourse and metaphorical discourse is the emotional response of the hearer. But one could argue that this was not really a linguistic or logical difference, only a psychological difference. For some metaphors this would certainly be true, for as we become accustomed to them, they do become part of ordinary utterances. Yet, another difference arises from the degree of confirmation that one has for these two types of language. Ordinary language rests upon well-confirmed experiences, usually so well confirmed that we call the descriptions provided by it literal. Facts that can be universally agreed upon can be described by language called literal, the ordinary language of everyday discourse. If a green table stands in front of us and we say, "There is a green table in this room," few can doubt the veracity of this statement, especially if they are present in the same room. An even stronger case can be made if one also points to the table while uttering the words "There is a green table in this room." That language can be employed to express the literal arises from the ostensive instances by which children learn languages.[9] The first distinguishable utterances of children are one word sentences in which the word used is an object like mama or milk. The child connects the word with the object when the adult present says the word and points to the object. Ostension is by no means unambiguous and the child goes through a period of hypothesis testing to see just what the limits are of the identification of the word with the object. When the mother is present, for example, and calls the world "mama" while pointing to herself, the infant could take the word to mean an article of clothing to which she points. Through a period of trial and error, however, the new language user comes to identify "mama" with the woman before him. But then he may, as many apparently do, identify "mama" with all women and have to learn, again by trial and error through corrections by adults, that only his mother can be properly called "mama."

Although not unambiguous, through the process of trial and error hypothesis testing the child can come to identify words with objects by means of ostension. Such an identification provides us with references that are literal in that they express universally accepted facts. Without such agreement, communication would be difficult if not impossible since ostension provides a series of well understood words upon which there can be agreement as to what they mean. Our account does not claim that language learning only takes place by means of ostension, because language learning also takes place through the association of words with other words. Children do, however, learn their first words by ostension

9. Cf. my "Ostensive Instances in Language Learning," *Foundations of Language*, 7 (1971), 199–210.

providing a basis for learning other words associated with these words. The mistake made by those who sought to reduce all theoretical terms to observation terms grew in part from the belief that for language to be meaningful, it had to be understood as ultimately resting upon reference. Language that could not be traced to references to objects or sense data in the empirical world was accounted as worthless. Then there arose the question of whether language could be meaningful that referred to fictitious objects.[10] But into that question we will not probe.

Nor would we want to claim that the literal derives from just that which our senses perceive, for errors in perception are far too well known. Mistakes can be discovered and agreement can be reached on why they occurred so that every act of ostension can be carefully scrutinized to find such errors and then to correct them. Ostension is not necessarily undermined by the possibility of perceptual error. Upon observing a table, we can move around it, touch it to make sure that it is not an hallucination and then get others to make the same tests before raising our fingers, pointing, and saying the obvious, "There is a green table."

By conveying what is literal, ordinary language provides a firm platform from which to judge what is hypothetical. Only if we have some notion of the ordinary and commonplace can we have any sense of the suggestive. Thus, a metaphor offers not only an unusual grammatical usage, but it also suggests experience beyond the ordinary literal sense of everyday life. And among metaphors, there are some that are more suggestive than others. Those that are most speculative and hypothetical never do become reduced to ordinary discourse, but remain primarily suggestive and hypothetical. At this time, we are not sure whether the tachyon will remain a speculation that can be neither confirmed nor disconfirmed or whether empirical evidence will be found for it. In poetry, there are irreducible suggestive metaphors and it seems unlikely that we shall ever adopt them as modes of everyday conversation. John Donne wrote, "Yea plants, yea stones detest And love."[11] Here is a case in which it is extremely unlikely that stones detesting and loving will be experienced by

10. Cf. Bertrand Russell, "On Denoting," *Mind*, N.S. 14 (1905), 479–493, and P. F. Strawson, "On Referring," *Mind*, N.S. 59 (1950), 320–344. The latter sparked a widespread debate about this problem and the literature on this subject is extensive.

11. John Donne, *A Nocturnal upon S. Lucies day, Being the shortest day.*

us as a testable phenomena. Certainly, when we look at a stone we may think of it as appearing as if it hated or loved, but there is little likelihood that we will ordinarily speak of "stones" as possessing the feelings of detesting and loving. There are numerous other metaphors like this one that are suggestive and appeal to our imaginations, but are remote from the everyday experiences of our lives. Literature abounds in them as do science and theology. It is doubtful that "force" as used either in Newtonian mechanics or quantum mechanics can be expressed in ordinary language. It certainly has an ordinary technical usage determined by theory, but this is not the same meaning as the "push" or "pull" that we think of when we use the word in everyday conversation. Similarly, we talk about God to each other, but we do not fully grasp all of the hypothetical possibilities for this term as suggested by various theological interpretations. The term "God" remains an emotional and controversial word because we cannot specify fully what we mean by it. It remains a tension-filled metaphor suggesting possibilities only some of which we can confirm. Not all of the metaphorical qualities of either science or religion can be reduced to ordinary language. That some of the suggestive hypotheses can be experientially confirmed in each is of prime importance. Without this confirmation, each enterprise would remain purely speculative.

The difference between ordinary language and metaphor rests not only upon the tension produced by metaphors and absent from common discourse, but also upon the speculative and hypothetical nature of metaphor. Some metaphors die and do become part of the language of the marketplace, but other metaphors remain suggestive and tension-filled. And the method by which metaphors cease to be metaphors occurs through confirmation by experience; when a metaphor suggests a meaning that is often confirmed by experience, it is widely used and the terms (or term) composing it undergo a change in their semantical meaning (new lexical entries are added in dictionaries).

The classification of metaphors that can be reduced to ordinary language through usage and metaphors that remain suggestive can be described by employing the labels "epiphor" for the former and "diaphor" for the latter.[12] An epiphor is a metaphor that achieves its meaning by

12. Philip Wheelwright, *Metaphor and Reality* (Bloomington: Indiana University Press, 1962), pp. 57ff.

expressing experience that is analogous to that of the hearer. Upon confronting an epiphor, the hearer will often recognize that which it expresses as being something of which he has only been dimly aware. His response is: "Yes that is precisely the way I feel," or "Yes, that is a way of looking at things that I had never considered before, but I am sure that it is right." The analogy between what the metaphor proposes and what the hearer has experienced allows it to become part of our everyday language. Dead metaphors like "time flies" all began as epiphors expressing experience that was confirmed by the hearers. A diaphor, on the other x hand, is a metaphor that *suggests* possible meanings rather than expresses meanings that are confirmed by hearers. Although the hearer recognizes the meaning as proposed by an epiphor as something that he and perhaps others have experienced or tested, he cannot fully confirm or disconfirm that proposed by a diaphor. After the initial surprise, an epiphor soon loses its tension as it passes into the ordinary while a diaphor may never lose its tension—it remains suggestive rather than expressive of experience and when interpreted literally always produces absurdity. The suggestion that a stone might love and hate always remains an imaginative suggestion. These two aspects of metaphor, however, are not mutually exclusive. There are neither pure epiphors nor pure diaphors. A pure epiphor would possess no suggestion and would be an ordinary analogy, expressing a way of feeling or looking at things that was quite normal and usual. Pure epiphors could not be metaphors for they would not produce tension in the hearer and their juxtaposition of referents would not be absurd when read literally. Pure diaphors which had no expressive element or analogy would be unintelligible. There would be nothing in a pure diaphor which we could recognize as analogous to our own experience. The newness of its suggestion would be nonsense or jibberish, for it would contain only suggestive elements and none that were expressive. Perhaps contemporary music would come the closest to a pure diaphor especially if we hear it as full of discord. But even here we can recognize some of the sounds, for the tones that compose the disharmony are tones that we have heard before. All legitimate metaphors have both epiphoric and diaphoric qualities; they must have some aspects which we can recognize as analogous to what we have experienced already and they must be suggestive of new experience or we will not feel their tension.

If all metaphors must possess both aspects, then one might ask why we insist upon classifying some metaphors as "epiphors" and others as "diaphors." We do this to avoid the misinterpretations that result from failing to distinguish between those metaphors that are more expressive than suggestive (epiphors) and those metaphors that are more suggestive than expressive (diaphors). Critics who wanted to eliminate metaphors as imperfect linguistic devices condemned them as being wildly speculative. In doing so they were considering only diaphors that could not be primarily expressive of human experience; we might recognize them as intelligible imaginative proposals, but they could not be tested. When religious language was found to be filled with metaphors, it was attacked for being removed from ordinary human experience. By viewing all metaphors as diaphors, these critics failed to take into account the many religious metaphors that are expressive of experience more than they are suggestive of it. Attitudes toward metaphor in science have been similar. The fear of metaphor in science arose not only from the awareness that such devices were imprecise, but also from the belief that they were speculative and not testable. Such critics forgot that many scientific metaphors are hypotheses that suggest possible experiments where confirmation or disconfirmation can take place. Certainly there are speculative metaphors that ought to be recognized as such; but not all religious or scientific metaphors are diaphors, many are epiphors that express experience more than they suggest it. This does not mean that all diaphors should be discarded just because they are not confirmable. There are diaphors like the tachyon that are now purely speculative which may well find confirmation in the future. Or, a theological concept like sin may be psychologically interpreted in such a way that we can understand it as expressive of certain dimensions of human existence rather than as solely suggestive of a highly speculative and artificial way of looking at the world.

The failure to recognize these two aspects of metaphor has resulted also in erroneous claims about the language of metaphor itself. Those who have interpreted metaphors only in their epiphoric aspects have insisted that all metaphors can be reduced to ordinary language. They claim that there is a paraphrase for every metaphor and they accordingly rob it of its tension. They fail to acknowledge the existence of diaphors that cannot be reduced to the ordinary because their mode of meaning is to suggest more than it is to convey experience. Others have looked upon all metaphors as if they were only suggestive or diaphoric and claim that metaphors cannot be tested by common experience. They say that the language of metaphor is a self-contained body of discourse where meaning can only be assessed in the context in which it occurs and not by analogy to our own experience. In its extreme, this view would prevent any metaphors from being intelligible for there would be no way for us to recognize them by analogy to our own experience. Although all metaphors both express and suggest, some do more of the former and others do more of the latter. Recognizing this distinction allows us to assess much more accurately just what their function is in a theory or in a theology. Epiphors largely express experiences and when confirmed often enough soon become part of ordinary discourse, while diaphors suggest possible experience which may or may not in the future be testable.

Another discovery about metaphor is that often it changes its status. A speculative diaphor may become an epiphor and then a part of ordinary language. What is suggested or proposed may find confirmation. When Einstein proposed that the speed of light was constant, this was speculative. Experimental evidence that tended to confirm it brought "light" to the status of an epiphor. Soon the evidence that the speed of light was a constant was so overwhelming and so widely accepted that it became part of our ordinary discourse. The term "light" itself as a scientific term still retains a tension as we find it impossible yet to give a description of it—some aspects are better described as a wave and others by the language of particles. "Light" does have a commonsense meaning, but this is not identical to its status as a scientific term.

A general account of the process through which metaphors may pass is the following. Metaphors are formed by juxtaposing two referents in ordinary discourse. This may consist of putting two words together, or taking an old word and giving it a new meaning, or creating a new word possessed of some properties which are familiar to us. The new metaphor seems strange in that it is an unusual usage and shocks us to the point that we stop and consider its possible meaning. If it is more expressive of human experience than suggestive, and if we can by analogy to our own experience understand the meaning that it conveys, then it is an epiphor. If it is more suggestive, and there is less analogy to our own experience, then it is a diaphor. After a while, it may occur to us that what seemed for so long only imaginative and suggestive really does express how we feel or think so that a diaphor can become an epiphor. Or, a scientific diaphor can find some empirical confirmation. Some epiphors are so expressive that we find them useful to express how we feel or what we believe so that they gradually lose their tension and pass back into ordinary discourse. Not all metaphors pass through this route, some epiphors remain epiphors as in the case of "light" which is still described both as a particle and as a wave; some diaphors remain diaphors as in the case of "stones" that "detest" and "love." Some diaphors may become epiphors as the tachyon might in the future if confirming evidence is found. Many epiphors, the dead ones, become ordinary language. What is significant is that metaphor need not be static as a linguistic device; it may well fade into ordinary language or it may shift from being suggestive to being expressive. Transitions in status take place as the hearer interprets the meaning of the metaphor and finds or does not find confirmation for it in his own experience. Consider the religious metaphor "God is love." For many this is a diaphor largely because we cannot specify very much about the nature of God. If God is a transcendent divine being removed from the world, then what would it mean for him to be loving? Could he be loving in the sense of human love and what kind of love, filial, erotic, or altruistic? Suppose a theological interpretation of this is given in which it is claimed that God's love is manifested in the love that believers show toward other human beings. This is advocated on the example shown by Jesus. If the committed do in fact act altruistically towards one another and towards outsiders, we may find confirmation that the metaphor "God is love" can be expressed in human affairs. The metaphor moves from being a diaphor to the status of an epiphor. But, it may well still be filled with tension if it is claimed that the word "God" in "God is love" still has some transcendent qualities. How is this transcendence related to altruistic actions? Even believers, although possessing a theological explanation in their interpretation of Jesus, may still find tension. For outsiders, the metaphor may still seem more suggestive than expressive although they were willing to admit that the "love" which the believers are exhibiting is certainly tangible. The next move may be to interpret "God" as a symbol for human love of the altruistic type. This would certainly place the metaphor firmly in the category of being an epiphor and, if all could agree, believers and nonbelievers, it might enter ordinary discourse with that common meaning. Believers, however, usually want to retain some aspect of transcendence in the notion of God so that the term "God" has not moved into ordinary discourse with this fixed meaning. Instead, it has retained a tension in that it cannot be described fully, and yet believers claim to have evidence for it in their own actions and in the past actions of other Christians performed in the belief that this is what Jesus revealed of the nature of God.

A term that does traverse the whole path may begin as a diaphor, become an epiphor and then a part of ordinary language. When the words "time flies" were first uttered, the hearer may have been completely bewildered as to how this could be possible—the metaphor was a suggestion, a diaphor; soon he realized, however, that there was a sense in which time did "fly" and it became an epiphor; then he found it a useful device to express his feelings of the rapid passage of time and so he and others used it over and over again and thus it entered into ordinary discourse. Epiphors that return to ordinary language become ordinary symbols in that they represent objects, or states of affairs or events. Ordinary language has this symbolic function of representation. Yet there are some symbolic forms that began as metaphors and which are fixed in meaning and do not, however, become a part of ordinary daily usage. These are archetypal symbols. Phrases like "water is birth and life" began as metaphors used in primitive rituals and have persisted in religion and in literature. The association of water with life became traditional and has lost its tension so that it is no longer a metaphor. We do not usually mean, however, life or birth when we ordinarily talk about water. This special symbolic usage is reserved for literary and ceremonial occasions. The original metaphor was an epiphor because there are some very real senses in which water does bring life. Without water life is not possible, water cleanses and prevents disease, and there is water in the sack containing the embryo. Expressive of a genuine analogy to human experience, the epiphor has persisted but has not passed into ordinary discourse. It is no longer metaphoric in that we are not surprised by the association nor does it produce absurdity when taken literally. Instead, it is that special type of language called archetypal—differing from ordinary discourse in that it is reserved for special occasions and used under different circumstances.

For those who claim that the justification of religious language is to be found in its symbolic nature, the acknowledgment that all language is symbolic turns their contention into a trivial one. If what they mean is that religious discourse is filled with archetypal symbols about which men should organize their lives, then we must ask why these former metaphors compel us to accept them as ritualistic centers for life. Since the archetypal symbol began as an epiphor, there are grounds for the association that the symbol makes, it is expressive about human experience. But what gives it special significance? Here those who want to reintroduce archetypal symbols into religious life must show just what it is that makes these symbols more significant than those of ordinary discourse.

Two questions that arise from this process theory of metaphor are: (1) whether every contingent statement is an epiphor; and, (2) whether every new technical term might be classified as a diaphor. Since most epiphors do eventually become so well accepted that they lose their tension and become a part of ordinary discourse, it might be tempting to suggest that no difference exists between an epiphor, expressive of human experience, and a contingent statement that can be tested experientially. But the epiphor that has lost its hypothetical suggestiveness and thereby its tension certainly is no longer a metaphor and actually becomes contingent in that it purports to express testable experience. The identification of epiphors with contingent statements, however, looks only at the end of the process and forgets that what allows us to classify a linguistic usage as an epiphor is not only its character of conveying experience that is analogous (expressive) to our own, but also a suggestion of how that experience might be viewed that is unusual and somewhat absurd. Those who claim that all metaphors can be paraphrased in ordinary language might easily identify epiphors with contingent statements forgetting that, not only diaphors, but even many epiphors cannot be fully paraphrased because they suggest hypotheses that are not fully testable.

While it remains true that many new technical terms are diaphors, especially those theoretical speculations that occur in new theories, many new technical terms possess little or no suggestiveness beyond their newness. Terms are often invented to specify measurements and these are stipulated in such a way that they do not produce tension by their odd linguistic usage or by resulting from a contradiction. We may be surprised to see a new term, but novelty alone does not produce the kind of absurdity and tension associated with metaphors. Technical terms that are diaphors suggest absurd possibilities by using common referents to suggest mysterious or uncommon meanings. Other technical terms specify testable empirical features or express well accepted theoretical characteristics such that we would not be tempted to classify them as either epiphors or diaphors.

Let us repeat again that there are no pure epiphors or pure diaphors; all metaphors possess both an expressive element, or they would not be intelligible, and a suggestive element, or they would not produce tension in us when we confront them. Some metaphors, however, are more suggestive than expressive so that they can be called diaphors while others are more expressive so that they can be called epiphors. The fact that there are borderline metaphors for which it becomes difficult to say which aspect, epiphoric or diaphoric, they stress more does not undermine the distinction. Even when the metaphor "Man is a wolf" was first used it not only suggested but it also expressed experience and whether one could call it an epiphor or a diaphor was not easily determined. Yet, such a difficulty does not prevent us from claiming that there are other metaphors such as the "tachyon" that are much more suggestive than they are expressive and warrant our calling them diaphors. After "Man is a wolf" came into common use, the analogy between human and wolf-like traits was well understood and it took its place as an epiphor. Yet, men are not wolves in every respect so that it retains some tension in the identification. The literal reading still produces some absurdity.

Labelling some metaphors as epiphors and others as diaphors, and realizing that with further experience a diaphor can become an epiphor and an epiphor can become ordinary language, prevents us from making some common mistakes in interpreting metaphors. The claim that all metaphors are reducible to ordinary discourse ignores the many poetic and theoretical diaphors that defy reduction, while the assertion that no

metaphors can be paraphrased in ordinary discourse forgets the numerous epiphors that can be tested experientially, many of which are on their
way to becoming ordinary language.

Thus far we have talked of the emotive aspect of metaphors solely in
terms of the effect they have upon hearers. The absurdity of a literal
reading of a metaphor produces its tension and this tension shocks the
listener. Not accustomed to hearing words put together in that fashion,
he stops and considers whether this is just rubbish, or if it really does
convey something that is either plausible or possible, or even just an
interesting way of looking at things. It has been sometimes claimed that
all metaphors are necessarily emotive and, therefore, cannot convey
knowledge. The first part of this proposition is surely true in that
metaphors do affect the emotions of the hearer, but we have also seen that
in the case of epiphors they may well convey information. Scientific
epiphors are partially confirmed and some religious epiphors find
confirmation in common human experiences so that the second part of
the proposition denying the possibility of knowledge in metaphors is
wrong. Diaphors do suggest rather than express and are thereby prevented from making knowledge claims, but not all metaphors are more
diaphoric that epiphoric.

Some metaphors, however, are emotive in a different sense from that
of just shocking the hearer by their strange juxtaposition of referents.
Poets do seek to express *their own feelings and emotions* through metaphors and in this sense a metaphor can also be said to be emotive. The
hearer may also be able to feel these emotions in the metaphor, or the
metaphor may be the occasion for his experience of a different set of
emotions. The poet may have despair in mind when writing and the
reader may experience disgust and repulsion when he sees the metaphor.
This is perfectly legitimate, but it does also raise the question of how such
emotive responses can be classified as knowledge. If the writer intends to
convey his feelings through the metaphor to the hearer and is successful,
then we can say that communication has taken place in that the hearer
has information about the writer. When this does not take place, the
hearer is aroused, but does not know the intentions of the author. Unless
the responses of a large number of hearers are similar to each other and
different from the writer, it is difficult to see the poem as conveying

knowledge. This is important for consideration of religious metaphors, for if they suggest different emotions to different people, then it is hard to see how they can be said to express knowledge about human experience. But, if they do express universal feelings that are recognized as such, it would be hard to deny that religious epiphors express testable human experience. These are not testable through perception of objects, but through communication of attitudes and emotions that people do possess. Not all religious metaphors seek to express feelings, but many of them do and their content is avowedly emotional. Scientific metaphors, on the other hand, tend to eliminate emotions as far as possible so that decisions as to whether a metaphor expresses rather than suggests can be made upon the basis of experiments in the realm of perception.

The metaphors that we have considered thus far have all been used to express hypothetical concepts in scientific theories and in theological explanations. Words like "force" and "positron" found employment as suggestive of various experiments while theological terms like "God" and "love" were used to express aspects of human existence that are not fully comprehensible. Metaphor can also serve another function besides that of suggesting possible experiments and experience or expressing that which is only partially known. It can present an hypothesis that is much more fundamental and comprehensive in its application. This is its function as a "root-metaphor."[13] A root-metaphor is the most basic assumption about the nature of the world or experience that we make when we try to give a description of it. Starting with the belief that the world is like a machine, we may then try to build a series of categories composed of physical laws which seek to explain just how it operates mechanically. Or, we may feel that the world is chaotic and meaningless and then we try to express this perception in novels and paintings. None of these assumptions are literally true; the world is not really a machine nor is it fully chaotic. However, the employment of a metaphor to express this most basic judgment about the world forces us to consider our surroundings *as if* they were machine-like or disorderly. The function of the root-metaphor is to suggest a primary way of viewing the environment or experience and this way of looking at things assists us in building

13. Cf. Stephen Pepper, *World Hypotheses* (Berkeley: University of California Press, 1970).

categories or in creating art forms that will express this insight. Our very notions of what is true and what is meaningful rest upon our underlying assumptions about the nature of reality. Without such tentative statements about the nature of the world, knowledge would be impossible, for we would have no way of organizing our perceptions into a coherent whole.

Contemporary philosophers who deny that there are any such basic assumptions undergirding a theory and claim that philosophy is a critical enterprise in which meaning is clarified ignore their own assumptions about language itself. Even Wittgenstein, who held that the business of the philosopher was to dissolve philosophical problems by attending to the proper and ordinary use of language, was aware that his notions of "language-games," "ordinary discourse," and "families of resemblances" were all perceptions about language that could neither be precisely defined nor completely comprehended.[14] These hypotheses provided a way of looking at language that told the investigator how to proceed in his analysis. Although such ordinary language analysts do not look for root-metaphors about the world, they do base their critical work upon root-metaphors about the nature of language. Such a view of language and its limits does prescribe a way of looking at the empirical world even though it may be negative in its assessment of the possibility of philosophic knowledge about the world.

A root-metaphor is constructed by considering a commonsense notion and then generalizing it by applying it to things, experiences, and events beyond those that are ordinary. Applying the concept beyond immediate experience, new categories are constructed to assist in the process. If the common-sense notion is restricted in its applicability, then it is quickly discarded, but if it does apply to many experiences beyond those of common sense, then it may be adopted as a legitimate way of looking at the world. For example, all men are familiar with their own bodies as a basis of life. Taking this concept of organism, it is possible to speculate on whether the entire world can be understood according to this root-metaphor. We know literally that the world is not an organism, but we wonder whether a system of categories erected upon this hypothesis will

14. Cf. Earl R. MacCormac, "Wittgenstein's Imagination," *The Southern Journal of Philosophy*, 10, no. 4 (Winter, 1972), 453–461.

be insightful and fruitful for an explanation. One characteristic of organisms is that they are in constant flux, they are born, live, and die. Certainly, the world changes and there are cyclic events like those of the organism. We note that higher organisms have intelligence. Does this mean by analogy that all parts of the world, not only lower organisms, but inanimate objects as well, have intelligence? If we are unwilling to admit this, then we try to show how such a category is limited and why only higher organisms have the function of thinking. With the category of "life" we may wish to show that "life" is nothing more than a special combination of chemicals and that the dividing line between animate and inanimate is not as obvious as it once seemed to be. And so the process goes; some categories will fit and others will not and still others will only partially describe all the phenomena. The root-metaphor is retained only so long as it provides a basis for a theory that we accept as explaining the world or part of it. No system of explanation founded upon a root-metaphor will be completely successful in encompassing all types of experience. Inevitably, there are competing ways of viewing the world, with different explanations. Some explanations better describe one type of phenomena than another and choices are made upon the basis of that elusive criterion of "adequacy." This is similar to the problem of deciding just why one theory is "better" than another one. In a few cases it is clear that the system of explanation does not fit the experience of most men and so is discarded. Taking a clue from the Freudian claim that dreams reveal much of the unconscious, one might be tempted to speculate that the world itself is a dream or an illusion. So empirically-minded are most westerners that this view of the physical universe is unacceptable even though for some forms of Buddhism and Hinduism it is quite normal.

For those who seek to explain the nature of reality itself, a root-metaphor may be applied as a world hypothesis as in the cases of considering reality as if it were an organism or a machine. Yet the scope of a root-metaphor may be much more limited, as it is in a discipline like science or even in a single literary work. The claim may be made that the root-metaphor of the discipline is also applicable as a world hypothesis and this has happened over and over again. However, this procedure often has led to severe disappointment when the root-metaphor used as a world hypothesis has been often convicted of distorting or ignoring much evidence that does not fit its categories. In the exuberance of finding meaningful categories that do describe phenomena in his discipline, the researcher may generalize beyond the limits of his knowledge. In the case of a single artistic work, the author genuinely hopes that the idea underlying his creation will have a universal quality. The novelist portrays characters that have traits common to us all, but to claim that all men conform exactly to his figures claims to much.

Both science and religion use root-metaphors as the basis for their whole enterprise, but the contents of the metaphors employed are different. To discern the differences, it will be necessary to look more closely at several types representative of each discipline.

A characteristic root-metaphor of scientific theory until the twentieth century was that of the world considered as a mechanism. Newton's mechanics along with the corpuscular theory that he and numerous others in the seventeenth century espoused provided many of the categories for theories erected upon the "world-as-a-mechanism" metaphor. This conceptual pattern viewed the universe as composed of a series of irreducible material atoms which interacted with each other according to precise mechanical laws. Although Newton admitted that there were gaps in this system of motion, succeeding mathematical physicists like LaGrange and LaPlace developed universal equations which they thought eliminated chance altogether and completely described the motion of all of the particles in the world. If one could establish the initial positions, times, and velocities of these particles, then it would be possible to predict with absolute certainty their locations and velocities at later times. This led to the belief that the universe was a closed, deterministic system.

So widespread was the acceptance of this root-metaphor and its systems of categories in the eighteenth and nineteenth centuries that men began to think of the universe as actually having this kind of deterministic reality. Theologians were so convinced of this world view that they sought to relate the mechanical order perceived in the world to theology. Their favorite device for doing this was the notion of a creator God who had designed the world with a purpose in similar fashion to the way in which a mechanic would build a machine.

When Einstein's special theory of relativity replaced the classical concept of mechanics, a great revolutionary shock was felt in the scientific world. Those who took Newtonian mechanics in its later formulations as the absolute description of the world had forgotten that all scientific theories have a tentative status. They forgot that the concept of the world as a mechanism was a root-metaphor, a suggestive way of viewing the world and not necessarily conclusive.

Although the root-metaphor of the world-as-a-mechanism was overthrown by the advent of relativity theory, its generalization into a world hypothesis had produced a reaction against this world view in the form of the nineteenth century romantic poets. Looking back to the heyday of mechanism, Whitehead noted that scientists of that ilk could have learned from poets like Wordsworth and Coleridge not only that such a conception of the world left no room for "feeling," but that it also assumed a separation between the knower and the known.[15] It was not only Einstein who claimed that the position and perspective of the subject affected his perception of the object.

The road to Einstein's achievement had been prepared by physicists like Ernst Mach who had demonstrated many of the internal inconsistencies within Newtonian theory. In doing this, Mach and others were proposing an alternative root-metaphor. Instead of mechanism, they were advocating science as mathematics. Viewing the world as mathematical in nature is an ancient root-metaphor dating back at least to the early Greeks with their preoccupation with geometry and numbers. Through the centuries, the inheritance of Euclid has been to use deduction as the basis of all reasoning. Spinoza's *Ethics* is a well known attempt to philosophize utilizing the deductive method of geometry. The Pythagorean assumption that the world can be represented by numbers also remains with us today. Few would take the metaphor the-world-is-mathematical literally for that would all too obviously produce an absurdity, but it often does achieve a dogmatic status when defenders of this view claim that theories can only be composed of mathematics and that models or conceptual patterns which employ nonmathematical terms are illegitimate. Mach and Duhem both objected to theories which borrowed terms from the empirical world to build their structures. Their assertion

15. Alfred North Whitehead, *Science and the Modern World* (New York: Macmillan, 1926), ch. 5.

was that the mathematical edifices of science properly represented the empirical world as confirmed by experiments.

A vastly different root-metaphor that we have already mentioned and which has been used in the construction of scientific theories is the conception of the world-as-an-organism. This is an ancient metaphor often used by primitive peoples in their mythology, but still used today, especially by those committed to a neo-evolutionary position. The process of evolution from inorganic to organic and then from relatively simple to relatively complex beings culminating in man and his society can be viewed as the development of an organism. The dividing line between organic and inorganic is almost impossible to make, especially with the recent successful analyses of DNA into its helical structure of triplet groupings of amino acids. Because of its earlier acknowledged association with mythology, few today take the-world-as-organism as more than an interesting metaphor. But the related metaphor of the world-as-process has received more serious attention. In the nineteenth century, Herbert Spencer's application of evolution to ethics and social behavior rested upon the conviction that evolution was real and not just a tentative theory. And this belief continues as most educated people do affirm the reality of evolution in a way that is close to mythical.

Perhaps the most widespread religious root-metaphor until the rise of modern science was the presumption that religion was founded on objective, miraculous, divine occurrences. This assumption was allied with the notion that the Bible was literally true and miracles were to be believed to have been witnessed conclusively. For centuries the biblical stories were considered to be the supreme truth. Two forces undermined the status which the metaphor religion-is-the-objective-truth-in-the-Bible had occupied for so long. Both the rise of modern science with its rational explanations of natural events and the discovery of the nature of biblical literature brought about a series of changes in the root-metaphors used by religion.

For many, the shift was to theologies erected upon the root-metaphor of religion as the experience-of-the-divine-in-human-life. Although Schleiermacher was the foremost modern exponent of this view, religious experience had been a part of the Christian tradition (and other traditions) for centuries. In the West, Christians looked to religious experience as the confirmation of their beliefs whether biblically founded or given to them in the life of the church. The tension in this metaphor is well known. The experience is said to point beyond itself to a being unavailable directly. If the metaphor is taken literally, then it reduces religion to human experience alone.

A related root-metaphor is: religion-is-personal-experience. This metaphor is used to defend religious experience from the attacks made upon it by philosophers, psychologists, and sociologists. If religion really is personal and related to the language of " I," then it is unfair to criticize it with third person arguments.[16] It is difficult to convince a mystic that he is wrong since he can always claim that his experience is self-authenticating. If you try his methods and do not achieve the same results, he can retort, "Keep trying and maybe you will have the experience and see the truth." This root-metaphor is different from the others that have been discussed in that it is more suggestive that it is expressive of human experience. Few people do, in fact, have mystical experiences. It is a diaphor for most rather than an epiphor and root-metaphors must have a major epiphoric quality to them if they are to serve as cornerstones for the erection of conceptual structures. If they do not, then the theories developed will have extremely limited ranges and in the extreme will be applicable only to the one individual who has had the vision.

The root-metaphors of both science and religion involve human experience. When the scientist starts with the assumption that the world is mathematical, he knows that this is not literally true, but that it is an hypothesis which will produce enormously fruitful results in scientific theories. The successes of his predictions as confirmed by experiments convince him that he was correct in making this assumption. The theologian may similarly know that the metaphor of religion-is-the-divine-in-human-life is not completely correct as he wishes to retain the notion that God is also transcendent, but if this root-metaphor yields a theology influencing human actions, then he feels confirmed in his adoption of it.

That science as well as theology rests upon tentative and hypothetical metaphors may be disturbing to those who have always believed that it

16. Dallas M. High, *Language, Persons and Belief* (New York: Oxford University Press, 1967), pp. 146ff.

was only religion that could be considered to be speculative while they held science to be erected upon the solid foundation of concrete fact. But science properly done never claims to be infallible and dogmatic; scientists are always willing to consider new evidence and formulate new theories. Sometimes the nature of the new theory is so radical a departure from the old that an entirely new way of viewing the world is necessary so that a new root-metaphor is selected and an old one discarded. Among theologians, it was only after the root-metaphor of religion as divine-miraculous-occurrences had been overthrown that the tentative and speculative status of the discipline came to be recognized. Some theologians still tend to be dogmatic, basing their attitude upon the earlier notion that religion was in fact objective. Objectivity, however, for both science and religion always involves the subject as he selects the aspects of human experience from which he will make, by analogy, assumptions about the nature of the world and human experience. These analogies expressed in root-metaphors then influence the way in which his explanations are constructed to describe the world and his experience in it. The categories selected and his theory of truth all must be in accord with the basic way of looking at the world that the root-metaphor provides.

Without the language of metaphor neither science nor religion could flourish. Both disciplines are "metaphoric" in the sense that they are erected upon the foundations of root-metaphors. Such hypotheses about the nature of the world and human experience are epiphoric in that they were conceived of by analogy to the personal knowledge of the inventor. They are also diaphoric in that they suggest ways of viewing things that are not literally true. But, science and religion are "metaphoric" in another sense as well. Each enterprise utilizes individual metaphors to convey ideas about the unknown. Old scientific terms that change their meanings in new theories are necessarily metaphoric. Theological terms must also speculate about ideas that are not fully known. In each case, legitimate metaphors must have some epiphoric content; they must be accessible by analogy to what we already have perceived or known. But they may also be diaphoric in that they offer new ways of understanding which we can test in experiment or in our experiences. Confirmation of these speculations may bring the metaphor into ordinary discourse as we become familiar with its meaning. In several ways, the process of metaphor that begins with ordinary language and moves to diaphor, and then to epiphor, and finally back to ordinary discourse is a reflection of the process of scientific and theological activity. Scientists are ever finding new data and offering new theories only to have them supplanted by even newer theories, while theologians are constantly rewriting theology in light of new understandings about human existence. Although the language of metaphor is not restricted to science and religion, it is essential for both. And while the content of metaphors and root-metaphors is different for each discipline, the function of metaphor in each is similar. Religious language may indeed employ different words than science, but the way in which it does so is identical.

IV

The language of myth

Myth is the mistaken attribution of reality to a diaphoric metaphor. As such, the language of myth arises out of the language of metaphor, for myth without metaphor is impossible.[1] And myth is possible in any realm of human endeavor where metaphor is employed. Not only do we find myths among primitive peoples and in the modern social and political realm, but they are also present in contemporary science. To talk about scientific myths may shock us because men have traditionally assumed a dichotomy between science and myth. The belief has been prevalent that science supercedes mythical thinking and that science views the world in a completely different way. The definition of myth proposed here, however, overturns these traditional assumptions by conceiving of myth as a universal linguistic phenomenon rather than as a story limited by time, space, or a special vocabulary. To assume that scientific explanations are absolute and final forgets that science changes drastically and that what may be an established theory today may be superceded within as short a time as a generation. Overconfidence in the success of science prevents many from acknowledging that modern theories may perform the same explanatory functions (albeit in a vastly different way) as stories about the gods did in earlier times. To claim finality for a tentative scientific theory is to create a myth, and that act of myth-making is no different from believing that the gods really did create the world by hacking the body of a fallen warrior into pieces. The contents of the two myths are dissimilar; the one is filled with mathematical symbols and references to empirical

1. Cf. Colin M. Turbayne, *The Myth of Metaphor*, revised edition (Columbia: University of South Carolina Press, 1970). Turbayne briefly notes that metaphors can become myths (pp. 18–20 and 59–60). He is more anxious, however, to demonstrate how to uncover hidden metaphors that may have beguiled us. He does not want one to discard metaphors, only to become aware of them. We are after the same aim, but develop our notion of myth as the consequence of taking suggestive metaphors literally. Other standard works on myth against which our position stands are: Richard Chase, *The Quest for Myth* (Baton Rouge: Louisiana State University Press, 1949); *Myth and*

tests, while the other is filled with descriptions of legendary heroes and deities. Contemporary men rightly assume that modern scientific explanations are superior to stories about deities as descriptions of how the world operates, for we have accumulated more corroboratory evidence for the former that also falsifies the latter. Furthermore, science is rational and predicts empirically testable events while ancient stories associate ideas in what seems to us a fanciful manner. Nor can one offer intersubjective empirical tests to confirm or disconfirm the features of primitive and ancient myths. Granting these differences between religious myths and modern scientific theories still does not excuse science from indictment as a myth-making enterprise when finality is claimed for scientific explanations since such claims lead to the formation of myths.

The reasons that men accept myths can be found in their beliefs that myths do describe *the actual state of the world*. This is the explanatory function of a myth. Without confidence that myths do, in fact, depict accurately the nature of reality, men would not adhere to the moral and ritual demands incorporated in myths. The difference between the stories which the Vedas offer for the creation of the world and the theories of modern science about the origin of the world may seem vast, so vast that we want to call the former superstitious and the latter a rational explanation. Yet, for primitive men, myths were the only explanations they had of how the major molecular substances of our universe may have come to control nature by sacrificial acts. And, we also attempt to manipulate the world in light of our scientific theories. Telescopes, radio telescopes, and space capsules are built and experiments are conducted to demonstrate how the major molecular substances of our universe might have come to be. All of this demands a socio-political organization to accomplish these ends and produces unexpected practical results in technology. From the point of view of another thousand years, our theories may seem superstitious and the institutions that produced them misdirected. Future

---

Mythmaking, ed. Henry A. Murray (New York: George Braziller, 1960); *Myth: A Symposium*, ed. Thomas A. Sebeok (Bloomington: Indiana University Press, 1968); Bronislaw Malinowski, *Myth in Primitive Psychology* (New York: W. W. Norton, 1926); F. Max Müller, *Lectures on the Science of Language* (New York: Scribner, 1874), vol. 2; Rudolf Bultmann, "New Testament and Mythology," in *Kerygma and Myth*, ed. Hans W. Bartsch (New York: Harper Torchbooks, 1961); Mircea Eliade, *Myth and Reality* (New York: Harper & Row, 1963); Ernst Cassirer, *The Philosophy of Symbolic Forms* (New Haven: Yale University Press, 1953–57), vol. 2.

archaeologists may look back upon much present scientific activity as empty ritual, research that had little purpose of direction other than to consume energy and funds. Certainly modern science is more rational than primitive man's stories, but to claim finality for present explanations ignores the fallibility of human knowledge and the record of the past where explanations about the nature of the world have been replaced over and over again.

By defining myth as the consequence of attributing reality to a suggestive metaphor, we have not given a definition which is limited either to the past or to a nonrational type of story. Myths can be formed unconsciously in the present by failing to remember that what we have given as an explanation is hypothetical and not final. That modern man uses reason for his explanations while ancient man used association does not alter the nature of myth-making. Each committed the same mistake although perhaps for different reasons; ancient man was superstitious and modern man overconfident.

Thus far, it may have seemed that we have talked as if every suggestive metaphor could become a myth. Myths, however, are not constructed out of just any diaphor at hand. Some suggestive metaphors are limited to immediate experience or to a particular event, and myths are usually much more comprehensive. Explanations do not cover just one event, but strive for universality in their comprehension. Even though a particular event or thing may be an instance covered by the explanation, scientific laws are not designed to explain one or two instances, nor are theologies formulated to describe a few occasions of religious experience. Myths involve creation accounts for theories applicable to a whole series of physical events.

Most often the suggestive metaphors that become myths are first employed as root-metaphors. These are the basic hypothetical metaphors that underlie a single explanation or a whole field of endeavor or even a description of the nature of the entire world. In creating root-metaphors, men make assumptions about the nature of the world and experience that stem from an analogy to their own experience. Successful theories build upon the basis of these metaphors, come into vogue, and are so familiar that the speculative metaphor upon which they were built is forgotten. The theory becomes a myth in that its details are considered to be accurate descriptions of the world and the world is given the reality that the root-metaphor only suggested. This is how men could believe that the world actually was created in six days out of nothing; they forgot that the author was *speculating* about how God could do such a thing. Similarly, Newtonians could be shocked by relativity because they too thought that the world really was composed of absolute length, time, and mass. In both cases, men had allowed a root-metaphor to beguile them into the creation of a myth. So useful were these underlying root-metaphors that they very quietly and insidiously became myths when their suggestive and speculative qualities were overlooked. This can happen in a single explanation or in a more comprehensive root-metaphor involving an approach to explanation itself within a discipline like science or theology.

One of the more difficult questions raised by this theory is: how is it possible to discover that something is a myth? When a root-metaphor and the theory or theories generated by it become so widely accepted that the tentative and hypothetical aspects are forgotten, few people are able or willing to recognize this as a myth. It seems to them more like an accurate picture of the way things are rather than a mistaken view of reality. They are willing to acknowledge that certain explanations in the past are myths, but deny that present scientific descriptions of the world could be myths. Compared to our knowledge of the solar system, confirmed by observations from telescopes and spacecraft, the idea that the motion of the sun across the skies can be explained by the Vedic story of Surya the sun god carrying the sun across the heavens in a cart seems ludicrous. That myths are always discovered and interpreted from the present seems almost self-evident. By the standards of modern science, the story about Surya is manifestly false as an explanation of apparent solar motion. Uncovering myths is, therefore, always a retrospective discovery. From our present knowledge, we judge past explanations about the world and human experience, and wherever men had claimed finality for their view of reality in an explanation that is at wide variance with what we now know, we label that explanation a myth. "Myth" was created in the past by those who held such an explanation, considering it as an accurate and literal account of the way things are. They forgot or were unaware that their theory was constructed upon the basis of a root-metaphor.

The difficulty of interpretation arises if we examine the present explanations from which vantage point we judge the past ones to be myths. Since we consider these to be the proper way of looking at things, does this mean that we have created myths in contemporary theories? This question is by no means an easy one. Myth has been defined as the false attribution of reality to a theory by taking a root-metaphor to be literal rather than suggestive. Now there is no way we can tell whether a presently accepted theory is *a false attribution of reality* until it has been replaced by another theory. In the future when that happens, of course, we will be able to decide that this theory which we now hold, if we hold it literally, is a myth. And so many theories have been discarded in the past that it is quite likely that many of the theories now reigning supreme will be replaced in the future by radically different ones. There is no logical guarantee that this will happen, but the belief that it will is also strengthened by the awareness that all theories are built upon a hypothetical foundation that is speculative and tentative. By taking the theories that we now hold to be final, we may well be creating myths.

Some would even acknowledge that all explanations accepted now are just as mythical as those in the past and that the job of scientists and theologians is to produce better and more adequate myths. It is argued that since men believe their theoretical explanations to be true, modern theorists are no less myth-makers than men of ancient times. Contemporary myths are considered to be better and more adequate in the sense of being more rational, using deduction rather than association, and more empirical, confirmed or disconfirmed by evidence in the physical world. This very positive view of myth, however, fails to understand the difference between taking something to be *literally* true and considering it *as if* it were true. Such a view misses one of the essential features of a theory, namely, its hypothetical character. Theories are proposed to explain phenomena with the full realization that many parts of the theory are unconfirmed and must be tested in experience and experiment. For most theories, there also exists evidence that is not compatible with its laws or assertions. The proponent of the position that "all-theories-are-myths" would say that such aspects as the tentative nature of a theory and the amount of negative evidence confronting it are measures of the adequacy of theories. Yet, the truth of a theory cannot be measured solely by the degree of confirmation that it receives, nor by how much speculation it possesses. Every contemporary theory is potentially a myth and it is best to prevent this possibility by understanding the speculative nature of all theories no matter how familiar they seem and how comfortable we are with them.

Looking at explanations in this manner forces us to talk about theoretical truth as something that may well be tentative. Truth derived from scientific theory does change with the introduction of new theories. For the scientist this poses no problem since he is by now used to the idea of revolutionary changes in scientific outlooks. But the theologian is more uneasy about such alterations in the contents of religious truths as he usually wants to build his theology upon a traditional basis. The history of theology, however, shows wide swings in the contents of theologies and even in theological methodology. Here, too, we find a tentative aspect in all theological explanations.

We do not mean to contend, however, that nothing can be considered as literal. Many things within our ordinary experience are literal in the sense that we can take them at face value without resorting to a theory in order to understand them. The language of our ordinary discourse expresses meanings that are literal. Either through ostension, the act of referring directly to an object or event, or by means of relation to other words that are well understood, the meaning of what we say can be established as literal. Ostension allows us to ground the meanings of at least some words in perceptions that are intersubjectively testable thereby allowing a common meaning.[2] Reference to objects gives the word a fixed and literal meaning. Other words that do not refer to objects depend upon their common use in syntax to establish their literal meaning. General words like "group" and "much" and adjectives like "small" and "happy" come to be understood by the wide variety of contexts in which they are used again and again. Although we may disagree about just how to define "small," we know in a given context what it means to say that something is small; we mean that a tree is "small" in relation to many and, perhaps, most of the other trees that we have seen. And even logical connectives, "and," "or," and "if . . . then," that are notoriously difficult, if not impossible, to define, are understood in the same way by ordinary language

2. Cf. above pp. 82–83.

users. In everyday conversation, the speaker assumes that most of the language that he uses can be understood literally and in such an assumption he is not incorrect, for his linguistic usage is grounded in words that refer to objects and events normally present and words with meanings established by a common syntactic practice.

Nonliteral language suggests meanings that are not ordinary and which stretch our imaginations to conceive of new possibilities. We have seen that metaphors perform this function admirably when their unusual juxtaposition of referents startles us into considering possible new meanings. We are forced to ponder things *as if* rather than as they are usually and literally viewed. We have also already observed that many suggestive metaphors come to express language so effectively that they lose their tension and become part of ordinary language. The language of the metaphor changes its semantical meaning to become expressive of the literal when such epiphors enter the realm of ordinary discourse.

In looking at the history of a theory, one may question what happens when it becomes well confirmed. Does a theory that is extremely well established follow a route from the hypothetical to the literal analogous to the metaphor that becomes ordinary language by moving from the suggestive to the well established expressive? Another way of raising this question asks whether every theory based upon a hypothetical root-metaphor that is taken literally must become a myth. Or, is there a possibility for some theories to become descriptions of what is literal rather than what is suggestive? Take, for example, the heliocentric theory of planetary motion. When Copernicus first proposed the theory, there was widespread opposition to it from Aristotelian and Ptolemaic supporters of the geocentric theory.[3] Utilizing Ptolemy's data, Copernicus proposed a different explanation of those observtions that was not necessarily any less complicated mathematically. Here was a novel hypothesis that provided an alternate explanation to the accepted theory. And Galileo was rebuked by the Church because he persisted in claiming that the heliocentric theory was an actual description of the way things really are rather than just a novel hypothesis. With the advent of the telescope and its use by Galileo and others, this theory received empirical confirma-

3. Cf. Thomas S. Kuhn, *The Copernican Revolution* (Cambridge: Harvard University Press, 1957), and A. C. Crombie, *Medieval and Early Modern Science* (Garden City: Doubleday Anchor Books, 1959), vol. 2.

tion to such a degree that it seems in our day to have lost all of its hypothetical quality. Larger telescopes and manned spacecraft have confirmed beyond a doubt that the earth and the other planets do move around the sun. The statement, "the earth and other planets move around the sun," has changed from a hypothetical statement to a literal one.

Such a change in the status of a theory raises a serious problem for our contention that theories become myths when they are wrongly taken to be literal, for we have just demonstrated that at least a few theories do legitimately become literal descriptions. How can we decide whether a theory that claims to describe the literal does so without making itself into a myth? How can we be sure that what we now call literal will not tomorrow turn out to have been based upon a myth resulting from improperly taking a hypothetical root-metaphor to be literal? About the only method available for such a judgment depends upon the degree of confirmation that one can provide for a theory. The heliocentric theory became so well-confirmed by so many observation statements that were literal in the sense that they were readily testable publicly that it lost its hypothetical status. In a similar manner, however, many scientists came to believe that Newtonian theory, which was so widely accepted and which seemed to be so well-confirmed, also was a literal description of the physical world. Newton's own statement that investigation should proceed by induction rather than by hypotheses added weight to the notion that the world view resulting from Newtonian mechanics actually did describe the physical realm.[4] In spite of the many speculative hypotheses found within Newton's theory, and even the contradictions which Ernst Mach demonstrated, later physicists did come to associate Newtonian mechanics with the correct and actual description of the world.[5] And the association was tempting since the Newtonian theory produced results that could be confirmed experimentally and so much of the theory itself was in accord with the ordinary perceptual experience of men.

4. Isaac Newton, *Mathematical Principles of Natural Philosophy and his System of the World*, tr. Andrew Motte and revised by Florian Cajori (Berkeley: University of California Press, 1966), vol. 2, p. 400. Cf. also Alexander Koyre, "Concept and Experience in Newton's Thought," in his *Newtonian Studies* (Cambridge: Harvard University Press, 1965).

5. Cf. Ernst Mach, *The Science of Mechanics* (Chicago: Open Court Publishing Co., 1902), and John T. Blackmore, *Ernst Mach* (Berkeley: University of California Press, 1972).

The overthrow of Newtonian mechanics by Einstein's relativity theory produced a revolutionary shock among physicists who had come to associate the notions of absolute space and time with the way the world really was. These men had allowed themselves to transform a theory that was still hypothetical into one that they assumed to have enough confirmation to allow them to treat it literally and they had thereby created a myth. How could they have allowed themselves to have been deceived? This was possible because they overlooked the parts of Newton's theory that were speculative and hypothetical and concentrated upon the large number of predictions that could be confirmed by the theory. When Einstein came to formulate his special theory of relativity, he did so on the basis of the contradictions that Mach had already discovered and not upon the basis of the Michelson-Morely experiment as is often believed.[6] Even Newton himself had come close to acknowledging the relativity of motion when he described the motions of a bucket and water in it as the bucket unwound from a twisted rope from which it was suspended. Instead of talking about the motion of the water relative to the bucket, however, he referred both motions to the same point in "absolute space." Such a reference is not only arbitrary, but contrary to our observation that the motion of the bucket is transferred to that of the water when the twisted rope is first released. But these and other difficulties in Newtonian mechanics were overlooked by those who took the theory to be a literal description of the way things were rather than remembering its tentative status.

Here, then, we have two theories, the heliocentric theory of planetary motion and the Newtonian theory, both of which were taken literally upon the basis of numerous intersubjectively testable confirmations, and we note that in the case of the former we were justified in our literal attribution, and in the case of the latter, we were not, for a literal attribution resulted in the formation of a scientific myth. If one is confronted with a new theory that finds widespread confirmation, before one can call it literal, one should scrutinize it extremely carefully to make certain that in spite of the many confirmations, it still does not retain

6. In his "Autobiography" published in the following work, Einstein paid his intellectual debt to Mach and others. Paul A. Schilpp, ed., *Albert Einstein: Philosopher-Scientist* (New York: Harper Torchbooks, 1959). For the detailed account of how this historical mistake took place, see: Gerald Holton, "Einstein, Michelson, and 'Crucial' Experiment," *Isis*, 60, no. 2 (Summer, 1969), 133–197.

speculative notions. For if one becomes careless and accepts a theory that is tentative and speculative as a literal description of the empirical world, then one may well be forming a myth, for another theory may replace it later and expose many of the features of the earlier theory as erroneous. Most theories, especially those formulated in mathematics, retain a speculative status since the physical world is not actually mathematical even though the mathematical expressions may generate statements that receive very accurate confirmations. With such theories we must beware the temptation to treat them as literal descriptions, especially when we find massive confirmation and become comfortable with them. Only when such confirmations *and* extremely careful examination of all parts of the theory indicate that no tentative parts remain are we justified in accepting a theory as a literal description of the way things are. At the same time that a theory receives widespread acceptance as a legitimate scientific explanation, unless these conditions can be fulfilled, we may create a myth by taking it literally, for only in the future can the judgment that we did create a myth be made when another theory shows our attribution of reality to a theory to have been mistaken.

By saying that myth is the *false* attribution of reality to a root-metaphor, we do not mean to imply that everything in a myth is false. What is wrong is the belief in the literal truth of the theory, the belief that the world really is as the theory claims it to be. There may be much accurate and useful material in myths and it can be worthwhile to interpret them both to gain insights about how the world might be viewed and to learn of beliefs which men held in the past. Contemporary theologians find the latter type of interpretation especially important for many of them stress theology as the study of human experience. They want to look at the attributes of religious mythmakers to see what impelled them to create such speculations in the first place. Historians of science uncover much information and insight about how discovery takes place by examining discarded theories. When these theories were widely accepted, just what was the evidence upon which they were based and what was overlooked in their acceptance that later was significant for their downfall? Such investigations call our attention to present theories where there may be much that has been swept under the rug or ignored inadvertently that could undermine well accepted explanations.

Certainly this view of myth as a false attribution of reality to a root-metaphor differs from the usual interpretations. In order to assess the degree of difference we shall compare our view with the standard interpretations and then turn to an examination of the consequences of our view for scientific and religious language. Much later we shall evaluate the results of adopting this view, which could be described as a stipulative definition of myth that urges us to abandon the more common understandings of myth.

One of the traditional interpretations of myth discovers its origin in ritual.[7] Myths develop as participants in the ritual seek to explain just how the ritual arose. Men may have gathered at a particular spot to perform sacrifices that were intended to insure success in war, or increased fertility in crops and children. Legends then developed as to why this location was of special significance; the gods had gathered here earlier or this river flowed from the body of a god in order to restore life and fertility to a land that had been decimated in a cosmic war among the gods. Linked with the ritual ceremony, these legends became myths. The function of the myth was to explain cultic practices. This position was modified somewhat when it was found that there were some myths— stories about gods and their involvement in the world—that did not seem associated with any ritual. It was also difficult to understand just how a particular ritual could become established without some prior beliefs in why the ritual should be of significance. What were the beliefs that led men to perform ritual ceremonies in the first place? Rituals were not established readymade and in a vacuum. They emerged in the context of beliefs about divine action and presupposed some mythical notions.

These modifications of the ritual view of myth led to a position that interpreted myths as cosmic stories about how the gods influenced various aspects of the world including the establishment of some rituals. For those who now interpret myths as fictional stories, this limitation of myths to "stories about the gods" offers ample evidence that myths are in fact the result of superstition. As men became aware of the "real" and "rational" nature of the world, they gave up primitive and childish beliefs. The rise of modern science marked the end of this type of mythology. But our notion of myth as the improper infusion of reality into a suggestive

7. As an example of the ritual view see Bronislaw Malinowski, *Myth in Primitive Psychology* (New York: W. W. Norton, 1926).

metaphor (diaphor) denies that myths are only stories about the gods. The explanatory function that such stories involving deities served for ancient man has been replaced by the explanatory function of science.

A second major interpretation begins with the premise that myth is an objective phenomenon and denies that it is a fiction or false.[8] Mythical thinking is a symbolic activity in which men try to represent the meaning of the world verbally. Myths are real in the sense that they have meaning for those who believe them. To assail myths as superstitious and unreal confuses their function. They are not intended in this view to be explanations of how the world operates, but rather express the meaning and significance of it. These objective myths contain recurring symbols called archetypes around which man organizes his life. Without such archetypal symbols, man will find life to be meaningless. Archetypal symbols include the concept of a central place about which life can be organized, and the cycle of life, death and regeneration. Usually in myths, there is a sacred place considered to be the center of the universe or the eternal homeland to which man must return. Aspects of sacral time also are mirrored in myths that depict gods who live, die and are reborn. Men who form such myths want to express the meaningful existence that they find in such archetypal symbols. A different dimension of human existence is revealed in mythology; here man finds purpose and emotional fulfillment that are not available in rational scientific activity.

Those who hold that myths have an objective reality different from the empirical world do not, however, claim that every detail of every myth is literally true. Local culture clothes the myth with its details and to understand the universal and archetypal significance of a myth it is necessary to interpret it. The best interpreters in this school will admit that the methodology used for interpretation is necessarily circular since they must presume that they know what the common elements of myths are before they sift them for the archetypal symbols that they contain. In other words, interpretation rests upon a prior understanding of authentic symbols, for if it did not, then any common element could be called an archetypal symbol. This is unacceptable since there are too many common features of myths that are considered to be trivial and not ultimate in the sense of being meaningful archetypal symbols.

8. Cf. Mircea Eliade, *Myth and Reality* (New York: Harper and Row, 1963).

This objective view of myth downgrades the explanatory function that myths have performed. Myths do explain certain phenomena and we have to admit that these were intended to be explanations even though we may reject them now as false. That certain major themes recur (archetypes) may mean nothing more than that most men have tended to have the same concerns in life about survival, life and death and that they have expressed these in explanations about the world. Myths are false in the sense that their explanations have been superceded by later ones judged to be more adequate and producing better practical results.

The assumption that myths have an objective status of their own is similar to the belief of dialectical theologians that religion is a different dimension of human experience than science. The consequences of this move are the same—the objective status of myth cannot be tested empirically and the assumption that myth operates in a reality completely different from science prevents the meaning discovered in archetypal symbols from having much relevance for science and technology. Such assumptions force men to live in different realms: the realm of science and technology and the realm of myth and meaning. Ironically, in the act of interpretation, those elements that are discarded in the search for archetypal symbols are eliminated usually on the basis of being contrary to the modern scientific world view. Myths are cleansed of superstitions and the remaining elements about human existence are retained as legitimate archetypal symbols. Although reason and myth are assumed to exist in different categories of knowledge, the interpreter employs reason. Such a move denies the fundamental assumption that reason and myth are exclusive categories.

Much closer to our conception of myth is the functional view of myth.[9] Here a myth has a comprehensive cultural role and is not limited to etiological stories nor to certain archetypal symbols. Rather, myth has the function of organizing the beliefs and practices of a society. Its stories justify moral and ritual practices. Primitive men behave according to a pattern because they believe in the mythical stories in which such practices are established and condoned. Myth functions to order and codify beliefs and moral practices; its main function is not to explain. Nor is the

9. Cf. Ernst Cassirer, *The Philosophy of Symbolic Forms* (New Haven: Yale University Press, 1953–57), vol. 2.

purpose of a myth symbolic as it does not create forms of reality but has a very practical and pragmatic nature. Our view of myth and the functional interpretation are alike in that in both myth has a comprehensive role and is not just limited to certain kinds of stories. We disagree, however, with the limitation of myth to primitive culture and the denial that myth can be an intellectual explanation. That myths affect the actions of men cannot be denied. When men accept a myth, they behave according to the demands that it places upon them. If ritual and sacrifice are demanded, then they will provide them believing that adherence to such a moral order will bring practical results. But the reasons that men accept myth can be found in their belief that the myth does *describe the actual state of the world*. This is the explanatory function of a myth. Without confidence that myths do in fact accurately depict the nature of reality, men would not adhere to the moral and ritual demands incorporated in the myth.

The limitation of myth-making to the past by functionalists stems from their assumption that myths cannot be rational explanations. Mythology present in the contemporary world is usually seen as a remnant of the past and useful only as it links us with our tradition. By defining myth as the consequence of attributing reality to a suggestive metaphor, we have not given a definition which is limited either to the past or to a nonrational type of story. Myths can be formed in the present by failing to remember that what we have given as an explanation is hypothetical and not final. That modern man uses reason for his explanations while ancient man used association does not alter the nature of myth-making. Each committed the same mistake although perhaps for different reasons; ancient man was superstitious and modern man overconfident in his scientific achievements.

The best way of seeing the consequences of this understanding of myth arising out of the language of metaphor is to examine a number of actual myths, both religious and scientific. Since root-metaphors are used both in specific explanations and to undergird the whole approach to theory construction, we shall examine two types of myth in each field—one dealing with a story or a theory and the other with the basic methodological assumptions about science and theology.

Among the most common myths in religion are those dealing with the origin of the world. In the context of their belief in some divine being or cosmogony, men seek to explain the origin of things by stories describing how the gods created the cosmos. The Christian myth of God creating the world out of nothing is the most widely known in the western tradition. Such stories, however, are not confined to Christendom, but can be discovered in most religious traditions. In each, the author who often merely records an oral tradition really does believe that things happened in that way. That he has created a myth and wrongly attributed reality to a speculative hypothesis is unwitting on his part. Those who believed these myths were unaware that they were formulating *myths* and it is only from a later description of the nature of the world that we can describe them as such.

A very early creation myth is found in the *Rigveda* where the origin of the world results from the sacrifice of a spiritual being called Purusa.[10] The characteristics of Purusa are not clearly defined; sometimes Purusa is a spirit that penetrates all of life and matter, at other times Purusa is given the status of a powerful high god who is named Prajapati. Whatever his status, Purusa is sacrificed in the creation story and the sky formed from his head, the atmosphere from his navel and the earth from his feet. The eye of Purusa becomes the sun, his mind becomes the moon, and his breath the wind. Two other divine beings, Soma and Agni, find their origin in Purusa's mouth—Soma being a god who inhabited an intoxicating drink that caused hallucinations, and Agni, the god of fire. The four traditional Indian castes are described as coming from the head, arms, thighs, and feet of Purusa. What we have here is the conception of the world as the parts of a giant who has been slaughtered. The most primitive root-metaphor underlying this myth must have been: "the world is a man." An analogy was made between the parts of the human body and the world. The eye sees light and brightness and the sun is similarly bright and the origin of light. There is the wind of the breath and the wind found in nature. The sky is lofty and above the other elements like the head which is above the rest of the body and capable of contemplation. When the giant is considered to be divine, the Purusa, then the root-metaphor is enlarged to be: "the world is a divine

---

10. *Purusa Sukta, Rigveda*, X.90, in F. Max Müller, ed., *Vedic Hymns* (Dehli: Motilal Banarsidaas, 1962), a reprint of Müller's *Sacred Books of the East*. For a general introduction to Vedic thinking, see Maurice Bloomfield, *The Religion of the Veda* (New York: AMS Press, 1969).

man." This retains the association between the parts of the body and the parts of the world, but it also entails that the universe is spiritual. All of the parts of the world are divine and should be treated accordingly. In later Indian philosophy, the notion is extended even further to the idea that everything is divine but not necessarily the physical world, which is thought to be an illusion.

Another ancient creation myth is the *Enuma Elish*.[11] In this Babylonian creation account the same root-metaphor, "the world is a giant," can also be found. Marduk, the warrior king of the gods, forms the world by dividing the body of the primeval mother god, Tiamat, into two parts, the upper one forming the sky and heavens, and the lower one the earth. The story, however, is much more complicated than that found in the *Rigveda* and seems to be a compilation of several stories each with its own root-metaphor as the foundation stone. The account begins with two primordial divine beings, Apsu and Tiamat, who are personifications of the seas along with their counsellor, Mummu, creating a pantheon of gods. Some of the divine children provoke Apsu by their noise and in a court scene he and Mummu decide against the advice of Tiamat that they must be killed. One of the sons, Ea, is too crafty and powerful to be overcome and he succeeds through magic—putting the world and the primordial gods to sleep through a spell—in killing his father, Apsu. Tiamat, the primordial mother, is enraged by this action and decides to war against the younger gods. They, in turn, create a new god, Marduk, "in the depths of Apsu," who is a powerful warrior and whom they engage to fight Tiamat. Marduk agrees to fight only after he has been acknowledged as king of the gods. In combat, Marduk slays Tiamat by causing the Evil Wind to enter her mouth and distend her stomach and bowels. With her mouth open, he shoots an arrow into her inner parts which completely destroys the mother of the gods. The battle ends with the capture of all of the other rebellious gods including Kingu, Tiamat's commander-in-chief. To give concrete form to the new law, Marduk creates the world by dividing the body of Tiamat into two parts. He then creates man from the blood of Kingu whom he also slays. The other rebel gods are put to work creating the royal and divine city of Marduk, Babylon.

11. Alexander Heidel, *The Babylonian Genesis: The Story of Creation*, second edition (Chicago: University of Chicago Press, 1963); cf. also Samuel H. Hooke, *Babylonian and Assyrian Religion* (Norman: University of Oklahoma Press, 1960).

The root-metaphor of the world-as-a-divine-being (giant) has already been mentioned as underlying the actual creation event. But there are other competing root-metaphors. In the opening act, there is the metaphor of "the world is water." Apsu and Tiamat are personifications of the seas and from them everything issues forth, the gods, the earth by the sacrifice of Tiamat, and man. Another powerful root-metaphor could be expressed as: "the world is both good and evil." Yet as we now have the story, the most basic metaphor seems to be that of the water as the chaos out of which creation eventually comes after the cosmic battle involving the conflict of good and evil. The other metaphors are not really the most basic assumptions upon which the story is constructed. Certainly, the myth as we now have it combines several accounts, but organizes them in such a way that Apsu and Tiamat are given status as the fundamental basis for creation. They are ultimately responsible for the explanation of the origin of the world.

Although the usual interpretation of the first creation account in *Genesis* is that God created the world out of nothing, the second verse suggests in a manner similar to the *Enuma Elish* that the waters existed before creation. There, "the Spirit of God was moving over the face of the waters." The *Genesis* story differs greatly from that of Babylon; God creates through an act of speech rather than by cutting up a fallen diety. Whether or not the waters preexisted, the basic metaphor seems to be "speech is a divine creative activity." There is an efficaciousness to God's words; when he speaks creative activity takes place. Another way of expressing this root-metaphor claims that "the world is speech." We know that this is not literally true, but we also know that primitive man believed it to be so. Rituals were carried out which depended for their success upon the proper incantation of words. And to know the name of someone was to capture his essence. Today, we can treat the world *as if* it were speech, for we know that many of our insights and perceptions are influenced and shaped by the words that we have available for expression.

In each of these creation accounts, there is a basic root-metaphor about which the story is organized. That the world is a body of water or speech is literally false, and yet this hypothesis is taken quite literally by those believing these myths. Each of these root-metaphors, however, rests upon observations about the world that are not wholly false. In some respects, the world is like the body with higher and lower forms, water is basic to life and life may in fact have its origins in the seas, and through speech we can construct knowledge and notions of reality. But, such insights when applied to the whole of the world go beyond the limits of their applicability. Applying the notion that the entire world is a body suggests a speculative hypothesis—it is a tension filled diaphoric root-metaphor and early men who took it to be literally true formed a creation myth. These myths certainly perform explanatory functions; they explain why the world is divine, or why Babylon is the royal city, or why one should heed the words of the Israelite God.

Not only do root-metaphors form the hypotheses upon which individual mythical stories are constructed, but they also undergird the entire enterprise of religious interpretation. A theologian may believe, as many do, that God is revealed in the scriptures. If he stresses a literal interpretation arguing that the words found in the Bible are exactly those spoken by God in the ears of the writers who faithfully wrote down every syllable, then he has formed a mythical view of religion. Such a theologian has taken the root-metaphor, "God is the word," literally. That the words of the scripture provide knowledge about the nature of God is an hypothesis. Those who claim that the author's words and God's word are identical must then face all of the contradictions and problems that arise from interpreting scripture literally. The sacred stories become final explanations of the nature of the world and man, and when they conflict with modern scientific knowledge are believed in spite of such discrepancies.

The alternative is to realize that the proposition "God is the word" *is* a root-metaphor that functions as an hypothesis when approaching scripture. Knowledge about God can be found by examining the religious experiences of the writers rather than by taking everything that they say literally. One can have knowledge of God's word only when one is aware that the writer mediates between God's word and man's word. To believe that the words of the Bible are literally and finally God's word creates a mythical view of scripture by forgetting the tentative character of the root-metaphor "God is the word."

Another root-metaphor that some theologians have adopted is: "religion is the experience of the Wholly Other."[12] Forgetting that religion should carry on only *as if* it were the experience of the wholly other yields disastrous results. How can one experience a being completely removed from human life? The assertion that it does happen, and that such happenings are paradoxes beyond human understanding is as mythical in form as the notion that Marduk created the world by cutting Tiamat into pieces. A being "Wholly Other" must be partially present in order for us to have knowledge of him. Yet to express this being's transcendence, we describe him as if he were "Wholly Other." By viewing such a root-metaphor as expressing rather than as suggesting the concept of transcendence, theologians can turn religious thought into mythology. The "God" taken to be wholly other in a literal sense becomes the chief element in a religious mythology where paradoxes abound.

At the other extreme, those who take the root-metaphors "religion is ethics" or "religion is interpersonal relations" literally can eliminate the transcendence of God altogether. God may be a symbol for human interactions, but this same term cannot designate a being that transcends man in the sense that he is different from human beings. For those who believe that religion is ethics, theological statements and religious stories take on the character of fictional accounts told to persuade men to behave properly. The conviction that a divine fatherlike God will reward virtue expresses a fiction that can be useful in urging the ignorant to behave properly. Skeptics may quite rightly ask why such mythical stories are necessary at all; wouldn't it be better to eliminate the need for such falsehoods by educating all men to the level at which they could recognize ethical demands on a rational basis rather than on superstitious grounds?

This second type of mythology arises when the root-metaphors underlying religious methodology are taken to be literal descriptions of the nature of religion. This makes the whole theological enterprise mythical in the sense that its most basic statements about the nature of religious reality are false. By taking hypothetical root-metaphors about the nature of religion literally, theologians made falsehoods out of tentative suggestions.

This mythical stance can be the reason for belief in individual myths. For example, those who hold that the biblical view of the world, with its

12. The reference to the "Wholly Other" is from Rudolf Otto's *The Idea of the Holy* (New York: Oxford University Press, 1958).

heaven, hell, and earth and with its miraculous occurrences, is an accurate picture of the way things are, may also believe, therefore, in the *Genesis* creation account. Historically, however, the *Genesis* account was formulated long before there was such a belief in the comprehensive root-metaphor, the-bible-is-literally-true. The *Genesis* account was gradually accepted as the proper explanation of how the world came to be. Individual myths may be believed because the root-metaphor upon which they are built is taken to be literally true or because the entire religious tradition in which they occur rests upon a literal rather than a hypothetical interpretation.

Scientific myths similarly are of two kinds: individual myths attempting to describe certain specific aspects of the world and comprehensive myths applying to the entire scientific enterprise. Like religious myths, they arise from taking a tension-filled root-metaphor more suggestive than expressive and treating it as an actual account of the way things are. Good scientists like good theologians are aware that their explanatory accounts are hypothetical and not final, but some of their theories that are still tentative become so well established that scientists unconsciously slip from treating the statements "as if" they were true to treating them as "true."

One of the most famous scientific accounts of the world relatively easy to recognize as a myth is that formulated by Aristotle to describe physical motion.[13] In this account, objects in motion can be in motion only if there is a force directly in contact with them pushing or pulling them along. Action or force operating at a distance is inconceivable. When an arrow is shot from a bow, the force of the individual pulling the bow is directly transmitted to the bow and then to the arrow to give it its initial movement away from the bow. Then to account for the motion of the arrow away from the bow, Aristotle found it necessary to describe the air also in contact with the bow as receiving the same force which it impressed upon the arrow as it moved along on its trajectory. Unless there was physical contact from force to body, there could be no motion.

Applied to the heavens, such requirements for motion meant that the forces which propelled the stars and planets would have to be in direct contact with them. Aristotle's explanation fulfilling this requirement

13. Friedrich Solmsen, *Aristotle's System of the Physical World* (Ithaca: Cornell University Press, 1960).

viewed the universe as a series of concentric invisible crystalline spheres directly in contact with one another and in which were embedded the planets and stars. At the center of these concentric spheres was the stationary earth composed of four concentric spheres: a sphere of earth at the center, then one of water, one of air and finally at the outmost periphery, fire. These were the ultimate elements of the earth and the four concentric spheres each filled with a different element was an ideal picture of the earth before motion was communicated to it. After the universe was set in motion, the elements became intermingled, although they still retained their natural propensity to return to their proper resting places—this is why fire rose and earth or matter always fell. At the outermost periphery of the universe was a crystalline sphere containing all of the stars which rotated about the earth once a day. The spheres between the sphere containing the stars and that of fire contained the planets. These also rotated, but Aristotle knew from recorded observations of his day that simple spherical motion would not account for the actual motion of the planets. The eccentric motion of the planets was explained by the motion of several spheres in contact with each other. Yet, these spheres were also in physical contact not only with each other (and contained the planet for which they described its motion), but also with the next set of spheres that described the motion of another planet. To solve this problem Aristotle speculated that there must be a set of spheres with the opposite motion for each set that explained the motion of a planet to prevent the communication of this motion to the planets on either side of this one. Unfortunately, this picture becomes complicated and spheres are being multiplied quite excessively. In the end, Aristotle's account of planetary motion included fifty-five invisible crystalline spheres. The substance of these spheres was called "aether" and all of them were in direct contact with each other. If it was assumed that this system was originally at rest, then there would have to be some explanation of how it got into motion and here Aristotle invoked his famous argument for the unmoved mover, an abstract principle that imparts motion to the system and is not itself moved by another agent. To allow that would be to develop an infinity of movers which Aristotle found unacceptable as contrary to his understanding of what was intelligible.

The root-metaphor for this theory is: "motion is direct physical force," derived from an analogy with the human body. When man impresses a force upon another person or object, he most often pushes or pulls it. Or he may carry an object. In addition, it is possible for him to set himself in motion. The fact that when we want to set an object in motion, we push, pull, or carry it is analogous to the notion that everything that is in motion in the universe must be moved by some prior push or pull external to that object. The last case of bodily motion, where the person initiates the action that leads to motion, was acknowledged by Aristotle as a different kind of motion from that which depended upon a direct contact with an external physical agent. In a number of passages, Aristotle used this self-causing feature as that factor which differentiates living from nonliving substances. If this were so, the root-metaphor that motion-is-direct-physical-force could not be literally true in all cases. Yet Aristotle built his theory of motion as if it were true and seems to have disregarded the possibility of autonomous motion by animate organisms when he constructed his arguments for the necessity of an unmoved mover. He argued that all things in motion had to be put into motion by another and that nothing in motion could be the source of its own motion. Of course, it was impossible to conceive of there not being a first mover that was not itself moved, for if one denied this, then there would have been no beginning and all things might still be at rest—a fact contradicted by our perceptions. Aristotle himself seems to have believed that his root-metaphor was a description of the way the world actually moved.

The Aristotelian myth that motion was always caused by an impressed force reigned in various forms for over a thousand years. Only in the seventeenth century with the development of Galilean mechanics was it finally displaced. As the history of the concept of "impetus" shows, this was accomplished with great difficulties.[14] Aristotle's root-metaphor that forces must be in contact with the bodies they moved found constant confirmation in the daily bodily experiences of men. And there was additional empirical evidence for this theory beyond that of our own bodies. Heavier objects did tend to fall and gases from fires did rise. The earth seemed stationary and the observations of the planet and stars could be crudely explained by the Aristotelian account. Seventeenth

14. Max Jammer, "The Conceptualization of Inertia Mass," ch. 5 in his *Concepts of Mass in Classical and Modern Physics* (New York: Harper Torchbooks, 1964).

century mechanics displaced the Aristotelian myth because it offered greater precision in prediction with its mathematical equations and because the hypothesis that the earth moved around the sun offered a more coherent account of planetary motion. Almost concurrently, new empirical evidence was found through experiment and through the use of the newly invented telescope that gave overwhelming support to the new theory. The Aristotelian theory of motion was exposed as a myth with the advent of a new theory that was more comprehensive, more coherent, and better able to predict physical events. The new physics came as a shock to those who assumed that the world really could not tolerate motion without directly impressed physical force at all times. And the removal of the earth from the center of the universe caused even more consternation because it served as the foundation for that physical structure. But when Cardinal Bellarmine demanded that Galileo view his heliocentric theory as an hypothesis rather than as a fact, he was right in the sense that all scientific theories are hypothetical, and wrong in that he, Bellarmine, also believed that the earth actually was the center of the universe.[15] So well confirmed has the Galilean hypothesis become today that we can speak of the "literal fact" of the sun's being the center of our solar system. We have already seen that a few scientific theories can become literal and lose their tentative status when overwhelming confirmation removes all speculative qualities that they possess. There are, however, many theories that are well-confirmed, but not so well-confirmed that they lose their hypothetical status, and to convert these into literal statements transforms tentative explanations into myths. Although the Aristotelian theory of motion found initial confirmation by analogy to the way in which human beings communicate force to other objects and beings, far too many parts of the theory remained highly speculative and later Aristotelians turned their theory into a myth by their belief that the physical world actually operated according to Aristotle's notions. So difficult to make is the distinction between a theory that has become literal and one that retains its hypothetical status that it is far better to view all theories, even the most confirmed ones, as still retaining some hypothetical aspect than to risk the creation of theories thought to

15. Cf. Giorgio De Santillana, *The Crime of Galileo* (Chicago: University of Chicago Press, 1955).

be absolutely true and later shown to be myths by the adoption of a different theory.

Just such a fate befell the theory of mechanics that replaced the Aristotelian account.[16] So dazzlingly successful and so comprehensive was the Newtonian account of motion that within a century the world was conceived of as composed of solid, impenetrable corpuscles that interacted according to Newton's laws. After Newton's equations had been given universal form by LaPlace and LaGrange, many scientists believed that it was then just a matter of time before all events in the world could be explained and future ones predicted. If investigators could find the initial positions and velocities of all of the atoms in the world and know the forces impressed upon them, then every event in the future would be theoretically predictable. All events were thought to be determined in the sense that causes in the form of the initial conditions plus the Newtonian laws could be found for them.

The root-metaphor of this theory is: "the world is a mechanism." Completely determined by the Newtonian laws of motion, the world was thought to operate as if it were a large machine. The spectacular success of this theory beguiled scientists into thinking that the world really was a machine. Again, the "as if" quality of the underlying hypothesis was forgotten. Space, time, and mass were all treated as absolutes rather than as hypothetical terms necessary for the theory. The difficulty of finding instantaneous points in space-time was considered to be a problem of measurement (measuring devices were not accurate enough) rather than a defect of theory. Similarly, mass was difficult to measure but was approximated as the ratio of weight to the acceleration of gravity located at the center of density of an object. Few until the late nineteenth century dreamed that such terms could be theoretical assumptions or intervening hypothetical variables rather than actual properties of the physical world.

We have already observed that Isaac Newton was not unaware of some of the internal difficulties of his theory. In his famous discussion of the motion of water in a bucket with a rope attached to it that has been twisted, Newton came close to the concept of relative velocities. He recognized that the motion of the water and that of the bucket were different when the twisted rope was released but he failed to define the

16. A. d'Abro, *The Rise of the New Physics* (New York: Dover Publications, 1951).

velocities as relative to one another and, instead, referred to them as relative to "absolute space." Newton admitted gaps in planetary motion when described by his three laws plus the inverse square law. He invoked God as the being who corrected these aberrations of motion. Newton also explicitly used several notions of "force"—one as inertia, another as a type of Aristotelian direct contact, and his notion that force is equal to mass times acceleration.[17] In spite of all of these admissions, however, Newton gave immense support to the belief that the world really was as his equations described it by claiming that he had no need of hypotheses. By *"Hypotheses non fingo"* he meant that all reasoning must begin with observation and from this empirical information one could by induction arrive at principles and laws. Speculative hypotheses were to be avoided and his rejection of them was aimed at Descartes, who had formulated a vortex theory of motion that seemed remote from the empirical descriptions of motion that men possessed. This stress upon observation and induction also led to another feature of the Newtonian myth, the de-tached observer. The objective world was thought to exist independent of the relationship of the observer to it. To a large degree Newton believed that he had found the actual laws of motion for nature by beginning with experiments and observations. This attitude coupled with the successes of his theory led many to believe with him that the world really was a Newtonian structure. So great was this confidence that the internal contradictions of Newtonian theory were ignored until Mach and Ein-stein brought them to light.

The greater the belief in the theory as absolute truth, the more shatter-ing the discovery that it is a myth. Acceptance of Einstein's notions of relativity exposed the mythical character of the Newtonian assumptions that space, time, and mass were absolutes. And so in accord with our common sense are observations that meter sticks do not change their lengths (except as affected by temperature changes) that the overthrow of these familiar beliefs boggles the mind. Relativity is so widely accepted that Newtonian theory is no longer seen as a competitor. The debate has shifted to whether Newtonian theory can be a limiting case for relativity theory (true for speeds that are slow in comparison with that of light).

17. Mary Hesse, *Forces and Fields* (Totowa, N.J.: Littlefield Adams and Company, 1965), pp. 136ff.

The Newtonian myth that the world was composed of absolute space and mass arose because men believed that the root-metaphor, "the world is a machine," as expressed in the universal equations of motion was final and absolute. The mistake of attributing reality to the hypothetical was discovered only when another theory replacing the Newtonian one appeared. The trauma of the overthrow of Newton and of other cherished theories is still remembered by enough scientists that some seem reluctant to infuse relativity theory with final and absolute truth. To hold relativity theory as a tension-filled hypothesis will prevent it from becoming another myth, but there always remains the danger that as we work with a theory day by day, we will forget that we must hold it *as if* it were true.

The Aristotelian and Newtonian myths arose when the root-metaphors underlying a theory of mechanics were taken literally. The theories that produced these myths attempted to describe certain physical features of the world. Another type of myth, however, pervades the entire scientific enterprise resulting from taking literally a root-metaphor upon which scientific methodology is predicated. At various times, investigators have believed that "science is description," or "science is experiment," or "science is mathematics." Science is no one of these methods alone; scientists describe, conduct experiments, and try to represent their laws in mathematical equations. Yet for the individual scientist classifying organisms, it may seem to him *as if* science were description. For the experimental physicist, science may seem *as if* it were experiment while the theoretician may understand science *as if* it were mathematics. When the scientist becomes so preoccupied with his endeavors that he forgets the "as if" part of the root-metaphor, he also creates a pervasive myth. Science as an organized activity has at different times emphasized various methodologies to the exclusion of others. Biologists, for example, until the twentieth century tended to look upon the proper activity of the investigator as description and classification. In the contemporary period, the emphasis in most sciences seems to be upon the construction of mathematical models to represent reality. The field of biometrics has arisen from efforts to apply mathematics to biology. Particle physicists go so far as to claim that what mathematics demands, science must provide, meaning that particles are predicted from the mathematical equations and then found in experiment. There is nothing wrong with treating science as if it were mathematics. Again, the danger comes from ignoring the metaphoric quality of this presupposition, thereby creating a myth. Pierre Duhem did just this in the early twentieth century in his insistence that all scientific theory must be mathematical.[18] He rejected models and empirical terms as illegitimate intrusions into science. Those philosophers of science who stressed the hypothetical-deductive nature of scientific explanation also tended to believe the myth that science is mathematics when they attempted very early to describe scientific theories as uninterpreted calculi of mathematical relations. Modern science since the seventeenth century has been characterized by the application of mathematics to the physical world, but to reduce science to mathematics ignores that it must be applied through a complex cognitive pattern involving experiment, metaphor, and hypothesis.

Scientific myths like religious myths arise from two sources. The first comes from treating a hypothetical explanation as a literal description of the way things are; the second source is the root-metaphor underlying scientific methodology. In both cases, an act of believing transforms the speculative into the mythical. Although the notion that the world is mathematical differs considerably from the story that locates the creation of the world in the slaughter of a giant during a cosmic battle, the act of believing that either description correctly and accurately describes the actual nature of the world is the same act. Scientific explanations are rational and empirically testable in ways that few primitive myths are; the confidence that our speculations about the world are the right ones differs little from the confidence that ancient men had that their stories about the gods and the world were true. Certainly, the reasons that warrant such confidence are not the same; a coherent set of mathematical laws that are testable is more rational than a superstitious and vague association of ideas. But our trust in the superiority of reason may lead us to the assumption that it is impossible for contemporary scientists to create myths. If a theory is rational, then how can it be a myth? The formation of a myth, however, has little to do with whether the contexts of the myth are rational or not. Myths arise from the improper attribution of reality to that which is only speculative. The discovery that scientists have

18. Pierre Duhem, *The Aim and Structure of Physical Theory* (New York: Atheneum, 1962).

created myths does not make their myths any less rational; it reveals that scientists have been unaware that myth can just as easily arise from *believing* a scientific theory to be absolute and final as it can from *believing* that some gods have engaged in a creative act. In either case, myth should be avoided by the realization that the explanatory account is based upon a suggestive root-metaphor.

The language of myth should ultimately be replaced by the language of metaphor. Myth arises from the false attribution of reality to a tension-filled suggestive root-metaphor. When men, scientists or theologians, realize that root-metaphors cannot be taken literally, they will do away with myth-making. It should also be clear that myths cannot be intentionally constructed. I cannot construct a myth for myself as the very knowledge that I am formulating a description of the world that is both false and purports to be an actual description of the world is self-contradictory. The conscious act of infusing reality into an explanatory account does not create a new myth for by such an action we realize that the theory we are using is hypothetical. Myth develops when we forget that explanations are hypothetical, not when we remember that they are founded upon a root-metaphor. Propagandists are successful in creating myths for others only when the masses forget that their slogans and views are the constructions of men seeking to influence them and believe that this is the way things really are. The propagandist, by his very act of creation, knows his explanation to be a fabrication.

Neither good scientists nor good theologians seek to be propagandists in that they do not seek to fool anyone. Yet, when they and others believe their theories to be an actual rather than a hypothetical account of the nature of the world and human experience, they have unwittingly constructed a myth. Later, they may see that they have created a myth, but this can only be discovered in retrospect when a new and more adequate explanation has been presented. Better to avoid the trap of myth by realizing that most explanations are to some degree hypothetical.

Myths are fictional in that their claim to be *the* picture of the world or human experience is false. There is, however, also much in all of them that remains true. From an examination of past myths, theological or scientific, we learn much about how others viewed the world; this tells us both about human existence and about the physical world. We try to ascertain why men believed as they did and what alternative hypotheses they considered in their process of arriving at the views that they considered to be final. By such study we can illuminate our own quest for explanation, adopting useful insights and avoiding pitfalls. The myths of the past should be studied, not discarded, and explanations in the present should be protected from becoming myths by an awareness of their tentative status. While the study of myth is enlightening, myth-making itself is dangerous as it breeds a false certainty. If the language of metaphor ever replaces the language of myth, men will be less confident of the knowledge that they possess, but more humble and more willing to consider various alternative avenues of investigation. Before leaving our discussion of myth, however, there are several objections to the view that myth arises from the wrong attribution of reality to a diaphoric root-metaphor with which we must deal. Certainly, myth described in this fashion stipulates how language should be used and does not purport to describe the traditional uses of myth. Earlier, we attempted to indicate just how our position differs from traditional interpretations of myth as ritual, function, and symbolic activity. But as a stipulative definition that urges a prohibition against the formation of further myths by suggesting that theoretical knowledge ought to be held tentatively, we are open to the following charges: such a view eliminates the partial truths found in myths, eliminates the possibility of creative interpretation, and leads to a possible contradiction by the very advocacy of the tentative status of theoretical knowledge.

We have already indicated that past myths do contain truths, some of them historical as well as others that convey information about the attitudes and understandings of the believers. If we were to eliminate myths in the future by refusing to believe that speculative explanations were real and absolute, the partial truths contained therein would still remain. Myths are not complete fictions arising out of the imagination of deluded men. Rather, they arise from man's desire to explain his experience and the only difference between a "myth" and a legitimate explanation is the claim by the advocate of a myth that his view is final and absolute.

If one were to refuse to make the claim that his explanation was final, creative interpretations of the scientific theory or the theology presented would still be possible. One can draw out the implications from a tentative theory just as readily as one can from a myth. What one cannot do, however, given a stipulative position, is to claim that myth reveals an objective and unique form of knowledge protected from the normal epistemological requirements. If interpreters of myth mean by "creative" a license to make special knowledge claims for religion, then our view does oppose that, for by defining myth as arising from a mistaken use of metaphor we have clearly rejected myth as a mode of symbolic activity that requires no justification for its disclosures. We reject the notion that words objectively reveal being by themselves and that in myths one finds word patterns manifesting dimensions of reality that are normally hidden from ordinary understanding. Rather, we see myth as a degenerate form of a quite normal linguistic activity, that of formulating speculative metaphors to express hypotheses and we understand meaning as arising from human acts of communication based upon language learning rather than from some recondite aspect of words themselves.

Some may object that we ought not to use the word "myth" at all for our definition goes beyond what many critics have previously described as myths. For those who believe that science employs reason and religion expresses feelings and that these differences can be seen in the construction of rational theories by scientists and in the formulation of irrational myths by theologians, our discovery that scientists also produce myths under our definition is abhorrent. These opponents charge that we have misused "myth" by stretching its scope beyond normal use. In reply, we admit that our definition covers more territory than many, but we claim justification for this extension on the basis of our theory of metaphor. In the examination of religious myths, one can find underlying metaphors, the root-metaphors, that were diaphoric and suggestive and then were taken literally to produce myths. In our examination of scientific language, we found a similar use of metaphor; scientists had built theories upon root-metaphors and then had taken these theories to be descriptive of the way the world really is, only later to discover that their theories were inadequate and were replaced by more adequate theories. If one claims that we should not call scientific theories myths because they are based upon reason whereas religious myths are constructed out of the association of ideas, then such a differentiation can only be made in ignorance of the failure of the hypothetical-deductive view of scientific explanation and of the extreme difficulty that philosophers of science have in demonstrating the "rationality" of contemporary scientific theories. Theories are often retained in spite of negative evidence and of known inconsistencies, and sociological factors like the methods by which theories are accepted enter into the judgment about whether a theory is adequate or not. Scientific theories may be more rational than theologies, but one cannot claim that the former only employs reasons while the latter only expresses the absurd. Both seek to give descriptive explanations of different aspects of human experience by constructing speculative explanations and both produce myths when they assume through familiarity that the explanation presently held offers the ultimate and final view. To claim finality in both cases generates a myth that can be discovered to be a myth only when another theory or theology comes along to replace it.

Still, the critic may grudgingly concede that scientists may have also produced myths but he may then object to our desire to eliminate myth altogether by urging scientists and theologians to consider their explanations as myths. Why not agree that all explanations are mythical and that the production of new theories brings us closer and closer to reality so that we can say that a new explanation is a better myth than the theory it replaces? How can a scientist not believe that his confirmed theory really does not describe things as they are? Or a theologian not believe that his description of God is real? To these questions we reply with counter questions. If one admits that theories and theologies are myths, then will one not also have to admit that they contain falsehoods since myths are never fully adequate descriptions or they would not be called myths? How can one both claim that his explanation is a myth and that it really describes the way things are? Earlier, we noted the impossibility of creating and believing in a myth for knowledge of its creation prevents the creator from believing in its reality. There seems to be almost universal agreement that the word "myth" connotes at least some falsity in its contents. Instead of accepting the labelling of all theories as myths and then deciding among them as to which most adequately explains the phenomena under examination, we would prefer to consider all theories as tentative reserving for the future the discovery that some statements within them may turn out to be false. Even the entire theory may be discarded when a better one becomes available. But to label an explanation as a myth now commits one to the view that it must necessarily be at least partially false. Another move might be to redefine "myth" by cleansing it of its pejorative aspect of "falsehood." But this would be to define it as a tentative explanation and would be even more contrary to common usage than our definition that defines myth as an act of belief involving metaphor. Although our definition is broader than many, it retains the notion that myths are in some way partially false. Notice further that our position allows a distinction among truth grounded in the literal (ostension), tentative theoretical knowledge based upon speculative root-metaphors, and myths demonstrated to be false attributions of reality to hypothetical explanations.[19]

Finally, what about the claim that all theoretical explanations are tentative? Have we in making this assertion possibly contradicted ourselves by allowing the claim to apply to the assertion itself? For if our assertion is itself tentative, then our description of how myths arise out of the wrong attribution of reality to metaphors ought to be taken lightly (tentatively) and if it is not tentative, then we may be creating a mythical view of metaphor and its extension into myth. Certainly, the account that we have given presents a theory rather than a description of the literal, and as a linguistic theory about other theories, scientific and theological, does it not also warrant a tentative status?

Most philosophical descriptions face this charge for when the criteria for describing are applied to the philosophical method itself, paradox and contradiction may result. The problem of defining "meaning" without presuming a notion of meaning is notorious. To avoid these paradoxes, philosophers have resorted to a distinction between the object language and the metalanguage. In the latter, descriptions of the object language are possible without application of the descriptive criteria to the metalanguage itself. If we follow this approach, then our definition of myth with its concurrent assertion that theoretical explanations must remain tentative does not apply to itself. It remains in the metalanguage. If one objects that such a move is arbitrary and occasioned

19. I would also claim that "truth" derives from interpretations of well formed logical statements but this is not the place to develop such an ontology.

only to prevent self-contradiction, then so be it. Better to prevent this contradiction by outlining the problem and denying that we have created a myth. Even if the assertion "all theoretical explanations are tentative" were allowed to stand as a tentative statement, then there would still remain the possibility that it could become seemingly so well confirmed that we would claim finality for it and thereby produce a myth, discovered later when we found a better description of myth.

We acknowledge that both our descriptions of metaphor and myth are theoretical, and we will assume that our theory about linguistic features of theoretical explanations is itself confined to a metalinguistic realm. Arbitrary though this move be, it possesses the virtue of prohibiting a contradiction arising from self-reference. As to whether this metalinguistic description should be considered final, I would claim that it should not for the very arbitrariness of the procedure allows for the selection of other criteria for description and, therefore, other metalanguages. The decision as to which is the best linguistic description of metaphor and myth can finally be made upon the basis of which theory most adequately fits the actual usage and which theory contains the least inconsistency.

V

Metaphor and myth in science and religion

Although we have talked about "the language of science" and "the language of religion," the languages of science and of religion are not two distinct and unrelated realms of discourse. Rather, these two disciplines possess modes of discourse that are members of the same family of language. Wittgenstein's notion that different language usages are related as a "family of resemblances" applies directly to the languages of science and religion.[1] Wittgenstein wanted to reject the notion that there could be a single essence for all language without, by such a denial, falling into the trap that language games must necessarily be exclusive of one another. Different language games resembled one another without necessarily demanding a single essence of language that would be common to all languages. His adoption of the metaphor, "family," to express the relationships among languages does allow some languages to be related to others by one common feature while still others may find a different feature in common. Ordinary language forms the raw material from which all different language games are constructed. But, ordinary language undergoes change constantly and encompasses so many different types of usage that to argue that it can serve as the common "essence" of any combination of languages misses its character completely. The inventor of a new language game takes ordinary language and modifies it to suit his purpose by means of various linguistic devices like metaphor with which we have been concerned in this study. In many ways, every specialized language possesses similarities to ordinary language; it may have a similar syntax and utilize numerous words in their ordinary meanings as well as suggest new meanings.

1. Ludwig Wittgenstein, *Philosophical Investigations*, tr. G. E. M. Anscombe (Oxford: Basil Blackwell, 1968), cf. paragraph 67.

We have already seen that both scientists and theologians take ordinary language and modify it to fit their special needs. Words like "force" and "particle" are given special meanings in the context of new theories. Such terms are initially understood because we know their ordinary uses and when a different possibility is suggested, we can use our imaginations to consider it. Some may object that science is more mathematical than it is linguistic in its theories, yet science must be more than mathematical in its discourse or it will be mathematics rather than science. There has to be a way to relate the mathematical equations of theories to the experiments which are used to support or destroy such theories. Science without linguistic concepts would collapse into an a priori mathematics unrelated to the physical world.

Theologians similarly employ ordinary language in special ways to construct their descriptions of human experience. Words like "father" and "grace" are given specialized meanings that are accessible to those believers who not only know the usual meanings of these words, but who also possess religious experiences that support theological extensions of the terms.

The languages of science and religion can be relatives within the same family because they both use ordinary language—in this sense all languages are related—and because they both depend upon metaphor as the linguistic device necessary to suggest new meanings. Scientists can talk to theologians and theologians to scientists, but how fruitful the conversation will be depends largely upon the relationship of the two fields. If they are distant cousins who have grown up in different countries, then their experiences will be very different and communication difficult, while if they are cousins who have lived in the same town, or are brother and sister from the same household, then the resemblances will be more intimate. To assess the nature of the relationship will be the task of this chapter. Our aim here will be to examine the structural similarities and differences of the two languages and only then will we be in a position to draw out some conclusions from the nature of the experiences that these two relatives have shared.

Stated very broadly, both disciplines attempt to describe different facets of human experience. The scientist wishes to give an explanation of the world of nature accessible primarily to our senses. This is not a simple sense data world, but rather a world of perception where the invariant features of the external environment affect the nature of the concepts which we use. Nature arises not merely as a construct of our minds, for the theories presented by scientists are the result of an interaction between the human mind and the objects of the world. Such an interaction is mediated by the physiology of perception, by the constructs of the theory, and by the nature of the objects under scrutiny. The theologian wants to give an explanation of the ultimate dimensions of life including value, meaning, and purpose. To do so, he must not merely examine his own feelings and beliefs in these areas, but he must also investigate the data of others professing religious experience. The resultant theology will be a combination of theological constructs and the data of religious experience.

Although both activities can be identified as conceptual endeavors, there always exists the nagging doubt about whether theology could be a "legitimate" conceptual discipline dealing with anything "objective." Science, by contrast, has objective limits placed upon its conceptual patterns by the external world. We have already met this objection earlier, but it will be well to review briefly the arguments here again. Theology certainly does treat dimensions of human existence that are "personal." "Who am I?" and "What is my purpose in life?" are questions that all men raise at some time in their lives. An exploration and explanation of the personal, however, does not necessarily mean that such an investigation will be subjective. It is subjective only in the sense that *subjects* provide the data which will be analyzed. Nor does science escape from the same subjectivity in that its objectivity rests upon the testimony of many *subjects* who witness empirical data (intersubjective testability). Science possesses a dimension of personal knowledge in its confirmation or disconfirmation of experiments.[2] Even this agreement may not be complete as there are different schools of interpretation of the data and even different perceptual claims. Scientists accept or reject theories partly on the basis of their prior sociologically and culturally established beliefs. The rub comes when theologians claim that they can infer from religious data a being that transcends man. For this being they may also claim an objectivity similar to that of the external world and at this point skeptics

2. Michael Polanyi, *Personal Knowledge* (New York: Harper Torchbooks, 1964).

level the charge of subjectivity. Feeling that such a transcendent being is not directly available in the way that perceptual objects are, they deny the whole religious enterprise. But this may be to throw the baby out with the bath water, for the theologian could also easily claim that such an inferred "God" was not *objective in the same way as the material world*, but rather a universal hypothetical construct (a metaphor) only partially confirmed and always tension-filled and mysterious. Traditional theologians have always resisted the temptation to reduce God to something like a physical object. Suffice it to say for the present that religion is not purely subjective and science not purely objective; both are conceptual explanations of human experience with the former stressing the personal dimension and the latter the external experience of man.

Scientists who wish to formulate new theories that are hypothetical and intelligible almost inevitably must resort to the use of metaphor. While a large part of such a new theory may be mathematical, still it must be related to the empirical world by means of relevant concepts and often these mediating concepts are metaphoric. Without the ability to formulate metaphors, the scientist would be hard pressed to offer new terms that were at once both intelligible *and* suggestive. Simple analogies would be intelligible but not suggestive, while *completely* new terms would be suggestive but not intelligible. The metaphor with its epiphoric and diaphoric aspects allows both intelligibility and suggestion at the same time. Those metaphors that are more suggestive or diaphoric than they are expressive offer the best possibilities for scientific use. As such terms find confirmation they may well become more epiphoric than diaphoric. Scientific language, like all human language, is fluid and may gradually or even abruptly change its meaning.

The need that theologians have for metaphor is so widely acknowledged that many interpret such a requirement as a weakness rather than as a strength. Those who have criticized religion have accused theology of being suggestive and unconfirmable while, by contrast, they have usually assumed that scientific language avoided metaphor and was expressive and confirmable. They have forgotten that every intelligible metaphor must have some expressive element or we could not understand it. The question is not whether religion can be understood and confirmed, but rather how much of it can be confirmed. The theologian readily admits that he suggests possible interpretations of religious experience, but he also maintains that his suggestions rest upon confirmed experiences. The religious experience professed by believers yields a type of confirmation for its expression clothed in the language of theology. Often, apologists for religion have been faulted for this seeming circularity, since critics objected to using experience as a justification for theological doctrines when the expression of that experience depended upon theological terms. How could one justify the existence of God by presenting a religious experience that was described as the presence of God? Had one not already assumed the existence of God when he described the experience that he had as "the presence of God"? The charge of circularity will stick only if such invocations are interpreted as proofs or arguments for the existence of God rather than as descriptions of experience. No circularity appears unless one claims that "God" is more than a symbol describing certain feelings, that God necessarily must exist with the evidence of the experience presented as a warrant for that existence. Such charges also forget that scientists are faced with the same problem when they adopt theory-laden terms to describe empirical observations. We have observed that some scientific terms loaded by one theory may be used in a neutral fashion by another theory. Such a possibility, however, does not extend to all observation terms for there are many scientific observation terms that are loaded by the theory for parts of which they serve as confirmations or disconfirmations. It is difficult to see just how theological terms could be used to express religious experiences and be neutral with respect to that theology in a manner analogous to the possibility for a limited number of scientific observation terms since most believers accept a single theology rather than a set of theologies, each describing a different facet of religion.

The theological need for metaphor arises from the fact that religious experience differs from everyday experience and ordinary language will not suffice to express that different dimension of experience. But this is no different in method from the scientific use of metaphor to suggest novel meanings in new theories. That "God" is a suggestive metaphor that cannot be reduced completely to an analogical symbol is not surprising at all when one remembers that a term such as "God" functions in the context of a conceptual pattern of explanation as a theoretical term.

What is surprising is that critics of religion have demanded that the term "God" be directly verifiable or directly falsifiable believing that "God" should have the same testable properties as a word like "chair" or "tree." The best that one can offer as evidence for the legitimate use of the term "God" always remains indirect. The religious experiences of men are rarely explicitly empirically testable confirmations of "God." Mystics may profess direct experience, but typically they cannot communicate this experience to others. They can only share their experiences with others who claim to have had a similar experience. If the nature of religious experience is broadened to include dimensions of universal human existence as in Tillich's definition of religion as "ultimate concern," then the question becomes one of why the term "God" should be given to this kind of experience and here we are at once engaged in a debate about theology as a conceptual pattern that seeks to integrate experience and tradition in a reasonable and coherent way. The metaphoric aspects of "God" become more explicit here for we are forced to consider new properties associated with that term. The conflict between the older associations with the term and the newer suggested hypotheses about its meaning produces tension. Those who are comfortable with a conception of "God" as an anthropomorphic ghost stoutly resist the suggestion that "God" might be better considered in a more abstract way as a mode of "being" even though they can present little evidence for their older conception except tradition.

Scientists and theologians both employ metaphors because they seek to present descriptions and explanations of phenomena that are not ordinary. Neither discipline would be content with a simple description of the things or events encountered in daily life. Both want to press further and explore the mysteries that underlie the physical world and human existence. This plunge into the depths of mystery offers enough justification for the employment of metaphors as they represent the unknown in terms of the known. A second warrant for using metaphors in science and theology comes from the fact that both disciplines present explanations that supercede earlier ones. New theories and new theologies are constantly emerging. In both cases, novel terms are required that are intelligible and suggestive. But there is a third and more fundamental way in which metaphor figures in both disciplines. As conceptual patterns of explanation, both science and theology are forms of human knowledge and they rest upon assumptions about the nature of the world and human experience. Explanations are constructed upon the basis of imperfect analogies between the knower and the known. These are the "root-metaphors" which we have already described at some length. They may underlie a single theory or the entire enterprise. Scientific theories have been constructed on the basis of the root-metaphors that "the world-is-a-machine" or "the world-is-an-organism." Many contemporary scientists and interpreters of science assume that "the world-is-mathematical." Theologians have assumed root-metaphors like "the bible-is-the-Word-of-God" and "religious experience-is-divine-revelation." Any conceptual pattern of explanation must be based upon some belief in the correspondence between the explanation and that which it seeks to explain. There must be some warrant for believing that this explanation is applicable to this experiential situation or else we would offer fantasies in place of theories. The root-metaphor gives such a warrant; although an imperfect analogy, it claims to be the most comprehensive description of the phenomena under investigation. We treat the data *as if* it were all like the root-metaphor because we believe that such an assumption about the world or human experience will yield fruitful explanations that can be partially and indirectly confirmed. Such metaphors become extremely dangerous, however, when they deceive us by their familiarity into believing that things *really are* the way they describe them to be.

Myths arise in both science and religion when men believe theories founded upon root-metaphors to be literally true. The explanation becomes so well established and so familiar that advocates of a particular view, scientific or theological, forget that the analogy upon which the entire structure rests is imperfect. The "as if" quality of the root-metaphor disappears and a myth results. At the time that men believe the world to be in actuality the way that the root-metaphor describes it, few even doubt that it could be any other way. Only later when a new theory supplants the old one do men recognize that what had been held earlier to be literal truth was really a myth.

Although myths have been most often associated with primitive peoples, religious rites, and sociological functions, if one recognizes the process by which a root-metaphor becomes a myth then scientists have also been guilty of myth-making. The *function* of constructing a conceptual pattern based upon a root-metaphor to explain human experience is the same in religion as it is in science. The priest in early societies who conducted an elaborate ritual around a fire-pit hoping to increase fertility performed this ceremony in the belief that the world actually could be captured in a microcosm and controlled by proper words and deeds. If fertility followed this ritual, then the beliefs found confirmation. If it did not, then the performance was searched for errors; if none were found, then an auxiliary hypothesis was constructed to explain the failure. Seldom was the ritual or the conceptual pattern of belief upon which it was erected abandoned. In *function*, contemporary scientific activity differs little from the activity of the ancient priest. Instead of fire pits, laboratories are provided where a prescribed activity takes place. Words are no longer considered to be efficacious, but the rules prescribed for the experiment must be followed scrupulously or error will ruin the results. The experiment may not be conducted primarily to change the universe (although its technological fruits may have that effect), but it is performed in light of a conceptual pattern of belief—the theory and its results are expected to confirm certain aspects of that theory. If it does not, then a search for experimental error is conducted; if none is discovered then the experiment is repeated. A series of negative results usually leads to a modification (auxiliary hypothesis) in the theory, or the theory may remain unchanged and the negative evidence duly noted and stored away until further research can explain why it occurred.

If we stopped our account here, it would seem that modern scientists are no different from ancient shamans. There is a crucial difference, however, and this difference allows us to call the work of one superstition and that of the other reasonable. Attention to the contents of the two types of conceptual patterns reveals this difference. The priest believed in a pattern formed by the simple association of ideas—imitation and words could control things in a magical way. The contemporary scientist, by contrast, does not accept a simple association of ideas as the basis of explanation, but seeks instead a deductive mathematical representation. He abhors contradiction and whenever he can avoid it, he will do so. His theories are neither fully consistent nor completely mathematical, yet he strives for both conditions wherever he can achieve them. Contemporary scientific theories are rational in that they employ mathematical relationships to link ideas rather than accidental associations. They treat the world "as if" it were mathematical and the results are spectacular; their theories are more comprehensive and yield more careful empirical confirmations than those of the shaman without resorting to fantasy to explain exceptions and negative evidence. The way in which the parts of the conceptual pattern are related separates the modern scientist from the early priest in their explanatory approaches to the world.

In this account, myth is not necessarily primitive. Although ancient men who believed the conceptual patterns underlying their rituals did create myths, there is no necessity for all myths to be the product of superstitious thinking. Myth does not only result from the association of ideas or superstition; it can just as easily occur when men believe that the rational and mathematical conceptual patterns that they have constructed as explanations are an actual description of the world. Men who associate ideas rather than ordering them by logic and mathematics do not necessarily create myths. Contemporary poets juxtapose ideas in interesting ways some of which are highly emotional and even at times irrational, and yet we do not accuse them of establishing myths. By contrast, the Newtonian myth with its absolute space, time, and mass results from a highly sophisticated and rational theory.

Fearing modern science, contemporary theology has stressed simple association of ideas in building its conceptual patterns rather than reason (logic might be more appropriate than mathematics for theology). Theologians failed to recognize that in destroying the old myths of religion, scientists had often replaced them with new ones. Theologians assumed that the use of reason would prevent the invention of myth. Nevertheless, we have tried to demonstrate that myth results from a belief that a conceptual pattern is real, and it does not matter whether that pattern is built up of the association or the mathematical interrelation of ideas. In both cases, myth should be avoided because it mistakenly treats a highly suggestive and tension-filled root-metaphor as a literal description of the way things are and we know that that is impossible because we do not have complete and absolute knowledge; knowledge ever changes with the advent of new theories. There is is no reason why theologians cannot build theologies based upon imperfect analogies with the world. But if theologians insist upon associations of ideas and encourage actual contradictions rather than abhorring them by relying upon logic, then they will be liable to superstition. At best, they will be like contemporary poets juxtaposing interesting ideas that do partially express our feelings. The contents of a root-meaphor do not result in the creation of a myth, but rather the way in which that material is treated. Yet this discovery does not permit theologians to erect *any* system of ideas no matter how fantastic as a description of religious experience, justifying the construction on the grounds that they will not treat it literally and thereby avoid myth-making. Such a procedure would be a flight from reason and a return to superstition. To qualify as genuine knowledge, theologies must be inferred from experience in a coherent and, wherever possible, a consistent conceptual pattern.

To deny that theology or for that matter scientific explanation can be fantastic in the sense of being self-contradictory or unrelated to human experience does not rule out the creative use of imagination in both endeavors. The formulation of any explanation no matter how rudimentary or complete, inevitably requires imagination. He who presents an explanation must first define the question and such delineation is a creative act for the problem must be posed in a way that suggests a solution. Out of a myriad of facts, the scientist must select those that he thinks are both relevant and fruitful for an explanatory account. He must rule out many facts as unrelated to the event that he wants to explain. He accomplishes this on the basis of some intuition or inkling of what the explanation will look like. A physicist investigating the flow of electrons in a semiconductor usually does not worry about the electronic activity in the water pipes of his laboratory. This he considers to be negligible both because such pipes are usually grounded and because the explanation of the one phenomenon differs from the explanation of the other. Selection is always a precarious business for the history of science abounds with examples of factors overlooked that later were discovered to be crucial for an adequate explanation. In part, the established theory tells the investigator what to look for when conducting experiments, but when he extends that theory by asking new questions, he may have to consider new facts as significant and this act of raising new questions about events that have been ignored requires a lively imagination.

Theologians are no different in that they too must pose new questions about traditional theological explanations. This is done in the light of new understandings of human experience and human knowledge. Selection of the significant in religious experience becomes inevitable when the theologian attempts to interpret religion in the light of what the contemporary period accepts as the canons of legitimate knowledge. Much of the history of Christian thought consists of a record of theological explanations devised to meet the intellectual challenges of the secular world. Reconsidering a theology in the light of a fresh challenge, theologians do not just rewrite the old one in terms that are more palatable, they investigate the religious data as well and often modify the nature of the theological explanation radically by selecting aspects of religious experience that had heretofore been overlooked. Rudolf Otto did just that when he picked the "awful" and yet "fascinating" aspects of religious experience as of paramount importance for his concept of the *mysterium tremendum*. Like Schleiermacher, Otto was trying to develop a theology that avoided the criticism that it was merely a series of intellectual propositions, or descriptions of emotional states, or an ethical system. His imaginative reconsideration led to his proposal that the ultimate data of religion was "nonrational" although always expressed in rational and ethical terms. And the selection of new facts or facts as significant that had been previously overlooked not only requires imagination, but often demands metaphors.

Selection is not the only imaginative act required by theory construction; those who seek adequate explanations must also construct fictitious and hypothetical terms. These terms should be posited only in a consistent and coherent pattern. Such terms give the theory a power and scope that it would not have if it were limited to terms that could only be operationally defined. Newton posited instantaneous spatio-temporal points that are really fictional ideals rather than terms that can be related to the physical world by precise measurement. With this concept in hand, he was able to solve his famous equations of motion and it was possible to approximate such concepts by measurement. Aquinas and Calvin talked about a universal divine law. Although they believed that such a law could be apprehended by man, we know now that such a concept represents a postulate based upon beliefs about the nature of God and that the evidence found in the empirical world only remotely approximates to that kind of concept. We recognize too much disorder in the contemporary world to allow the concept of natural law to stand as an accurate description of the way things are. What we reject in the thought of Newton, Aquinas, and Calvin is not their use of theoretical terms, but rather their claims that such terms are actual descriptions of the physical world. All theories need theoretical terms so that they can do more than just describe experience since the very nature of explanation is to suggest how things might be. Scientists who can creatively suggest new metaphors for theoretical terms and place them in a consistent and coherent pattern project science into the future of new explanations. And the theologian who can imagine new concepts for theological terms like God or faith forces us to raise new questions about the nature of religious experience.

Since theology and science deal with mystery—we will never fully know either the ultimate purpose of life or the ultimate nature of the world—the very act of giving an explanation will be imaginative and creative in both cases. To present a theory is to select factors from experience that are considered significant and to weave them in combination with theoretically posited terms into a tapestry that displays a plausible and coherent picture of the way things might be. The root-metaphor underlying the theory presents the basic pattern for the fabric while the facts (although theory-laden) and hypothetical terms compose the yarns. A creative weaver will use his imagination first to design a novel pattern with knowledge of what standard yarns are available. Then, if he is really imaginative, he may even dye some new yarns to add to those which are readily available. Finally, he will select his standard yarns, dye his new ones, and weave the cloth. A theory like a tapestry can be successful if it suggests the way that things might be; but the theory unlike the tapestry, if it is to be accepted, must eventually find empirical confirmation for its suggestions.

Theological weavers at the Council of Nicea were faced with the problem of how to relate Jesus to God in a fashion that expressed the divinity of the former without adding a second deity to the universe. Reluctantly, the Council followed the suggestion of Athanasius in approving "homousia" as the term manifesting this relationship.[3] Translated as "of one substance," in the Nicene Creed Jesus is affirmed as of one substance with God, the Father. Much of the uneasiness came over the fact that the new yarn, "homousia," was not a biblical word. Theological confirmation for this move was found in the belief that God had been actually manifested in a human form, Jesus.

The appearance of a new type of explanation will often encounter difficulty because it demands a new set of ground rules for what will constitute a legitimate explanation. Witness the objections raised to Darwin's theory of evolution by nineteenth century scientists who believed both that the time required by evolution exceeded that available for the creation of the world in existing theories and that the best theories should be mechanical.[4] Since Darwin's theory was not mechanical and stretched the imagination beyond conceptual limits imposed by existing theories, the initial tendency among many scientists was to reject it as an improper theory.

The form that a legitimate pattern of explanation must take in any discipline is, in part, a function of the beliefs of investigators within that discipline as to what constitutes a proper explanation. Today, scientific explanations demand as much mathematical rigor as possible while theological patterns of explanation seek to justify upon the basis of religious experience inferences to that which is beyond the human realm. In offering stories about the creation of the world and the nature of how the world operated, ancient man similarly drew upon a stock of existing stories and rituals that were considered to be acceptable as conceptual patterns of explanation. From our perspective, such stories are classified as myths since we have different patterns of explanation that seem to us to be rational while the older stories seem superstitious and fantastic. But for ancient man, such stories were no less an accepted pattern of explanation than our scientific theories are for us. One difference between the two arises from our contemporary awareness that theories can be superceded by later theories and that we must be extremely cautious about committing ourselves to any hypothetical view as the final and correct understanding of the world.

3. Cf. Reinhold Seeberg, *Text-Book of the History of Doctrines*, tr. Charles E. Hay (Grand Rapids, Mich.: Baker Book House, 1964) pp. 206ff.

4. Cf. Loren Eiseley, *Darwin's Century* (Garden City, N.Y.: Anchor Books, 1961), expecially ch. 9, "Darwin and the Physicists."

Another difference comes from our claim that modern theories are reasonable in ways that ancient myths were not. While ancient myths associated ideas haphazardly, we claim that modern theories and theologies associate ideas rationally. But just what does it mean to say that contemporary theories are *rational* patterns of explanation? If we claim that rational means deductive, we know that this is far too narrow as a definition for it ignores inductive procedures and we know from the failure of the hypothetico-deductive account of scientific explanation that such a definition will describe very little actual scientific activity for it ignores the changing nature of theories. Nor can we argue that confirmation makes modern theories reasonable for many theories that are now considered to be mythical were believed to have been confirmed by those who held them. Nor will induction by itself serve as a definition of reason. Causality presents another possibility for defining reason; modern theories are said to be reasonable because they offer causes in the context of an explanation. Yet, this will not serve either for when we ask just how cause and effect are related, we may not claim by strict deduction or induction for we have just ruled these out as definitions of rationality in explanation because they restrict the scope of such explanations unduly. If we argue that cause and effect are related temporally, then we must ask which one of a number of prior factors should be singled out as a causal factor and which ones ignored? If we assert that cause and effect are arbitrarily united by the constant conjunction of ideas, then we will be no better off than ancient man with his superstitious association of ideas.

We might put forth the claim that for a conceptual pattern to qualify as rational it must be intelligible. This does not mean that every citizen must be able to understand it, but that those specialists in the particular discipline are able to comprehend it. Even though a new theory be highly complex and suggestive, other researchers ought to be capable of understanding the novel hypotheses proposed. Yet intelligibility depends upon the context in which it occurs. The form of argumentation used in one field may not be applicable to another. Stephen Toulmin has offered the model of legal proceedings for arguments against the usual assumption that arguments must be deductive.[5] Rarely, he claims, are debates settled

5. Stephen Toulmin, "The Layout of Arguments," in his *The Uses of Argument* (Cambridge: Cambridge University Press, 1964).

by symbolic logic; rather, men offer warrants with qualifying exceptions for their conclusions. Time also enters the question for what may be intelligible as an explanation in one period may be rejected in another. The identification of "rational" with "intelligible" merely identifies reasons with what is acceptable in a particular discipline at a particular time and that does little to assist us in differentiating between justifiable reason and objectionable fancy.

Although intelligibility is not a sufficient condition for rationality, certainly it is necessary, because conceptual patterns that are not intelligible cannot qualify as rational. The first step towards accepting a theory or theology as a legitimate pattern of explanation occurs when we comprehend it as intelligible. And what we recognize does depend upon what we have been conditioned to recognize as intelligible.

Coherence is another necessary but not sufficient condition for rationality. If we are to call a theory rational, the parts of its conceptual pattern should fit together in a coherent whole. Coherence means that the parts of a theory are required by one another to perform the explanatory function. Consistency is a much stronger requirement than coherence, but to limit rational conceptual patterns to those which could be shown to be consistent would be to limit the scope of theories too much. Most scientific theories encompass more than logical or mathematical relations; they include concepts and relationships that link various parts of the theory and that tie the theory to the empirical world through experiment. To restrict theologies to a series of consistent propositions would be to rob such theories of most of their contents. Theological statements that are coherent with one another are extremely difficult if not impossible to demonstrate as consistent. Requiring coherence in theories enables us to see a pattern among the concepts for they must fit together into a whole. Coherence also provides us with a warrant to use Occam's Razor to cut off those concepts that are not required by any of the others within a theory.

Although coherence is not as strong a requirement as consistency, it should not be used as a justification for inconsistency. Wherever possible, inconsistency should be avoided; if two concepts are required for an explanation but are mutually inconsistent, then we should seek other principles that are not inconsistent to replace them. Without the further stipulation against inconsistency, coherence by itself would not prevent irrationality. Contradictions destroy theories by allowing any proposition whatsoever to be generated from them. The appearance of a contradiction should warn us of the inadequacy of the conceptual pattern within a theory. Some contemporary theologians have not feared contradiction enough and have produced theologies that are highly irrational. Scientists are more wary of contradiction, possibly because they are better versed in mathematics and formal thinking. They do come close to contradiction when they describe light as both a wave and a particle, but many see such descriptions as alternatives applying to the different phenomena of light. This dual description is accepted only because no better unified theory of light exists to overcome this problem. Theologians who have claimed that God exists completely apart from the world and also can be paradoxically present in it either are equivocating upon the words "completely apart" or have created a contradiction. And alleviation of this problem is not to be found in the assertion that no paradox exists since theological words present a disclosure of Being to which the categories of subject and object are inapplicable. The contradiction cannot be dissolved in an obscure and unlikely account of how subjectivity and objectivity are overcome by a vague notion of being.

A third necessary condition for the rationality of conceptual patterns is the absence of inconsistency. To require consistency would be to reduce theories to formal logics or mathematics since it becomes extremely difficult to show that all parts of even a scientific theory are consistent. It would also reduce the scope of theories almost to triviality as hypothetical speculations would have to be eliminated unless they were strictly deduced within an axiomatic system. Anomalous and ambiguous evidence would similarly have to be dismissed. Rather than requiring that all parts of a theory be demonstrated as consistent with each other, we require that the parts must fit together in a pattern of coherence in which inconsistencies are avoided. Inconsistencies will appear in both scientific theories and theologies, and whenever they occur we should seek to eliminate them.

Positive evidence must also be available if a theory is to be called rational. The source of this evidence must be human experience. In science, perception provides the primary source of data. Experiments are conducted and the results are available for anyone who wishes to repeat them. Even though the instruments used to measure the results are constructed on the basis of theoretical beliefs about the nature of what is being tested, the final criterion of objectivity still remains intersubjective testability.

That these four criteria of intelligibility, coherence, absence of inconsistency, and confirmation are not sufficient to describe a satisfactory explanation can be seen by examining a contemporary scientific theory like that of genetics. From the simple view of Mendel that genes were inherited characteristics, two types of genetic theory have arisen: transmission genetics concerned with the organization and transmission of information in inheritance, and molecular genetics, concerned with biochemical mechanisms that process information for cellular operations.[6] In these two approaches to genetics, the term "gene" has been employed differently, indicating that there may well be some incoherence if not inconsistency in these scientific theories. In the future, some hope, these two modes of "genetics" will prove to be two phases of the same human process, a development that would eliminate some of the tension and confusion. At the moment, however, these two types of genetic theory exist side by side, testimonies to the importance of confirmation, for to seek to eliminate either would be to fly from the mass of data presently available.

Theology and science both find confirmation of their theories in human experience with the former stressing the dimensions of feeling and value, and the latter, perception. Yet theology also manifests itself in actions that are perceivable and science forgets at its peril that what we see is directly influenced by what we accept as a theory. Religion is subjective in the sense that its evidence is largely found in the realm of the *personal*, but this is not pure subjectivism for the experiences found there are shared by many. Science is *objective* in that it is intersubjectively testable through a perception, but that is not to make it purely objective for the personal beliefs and feelings of investigators directly affect the nature of both the evidence and the theory.

Calvin's systematic theology presented in his *Institutes of the Christian*

6. Cf. James F. Case and Vernon E. Stiers, *Biology: Observation and Concept* (New York: Macmillan, 1971), ch. 13, pp. 336–362.

Religion unites subjective faith with objective interpretations of the world and history. Seeking a rational and coherent expression of religion, Calvin also sought to harmonize fact and value by making ethics dependent upon God's providence. And Calvin claimed an objectivity for his theology not only in its divine origin but also in its apprehension by men. Without personal faith, however, men could not be aware of the full extent of God's providence.

Accepting a theory commits one to creating a picture about the world with the extent of the picture's reference determined by the scope of the theory. Theories can be described as visual metaphors in that they see the world as *something* with that "something" given by the root-metaphor upon which the theory is constructed. Wittgenstein used the notion of "seeing as" to mean "noting an aspect."[7] When we accept a theory like relativity, we see the world as composed of the constant speed of light and of length and time changing relative to velocity. These are the aspects that we note. But we also might note other aspects since *seeing* the world *as* relativity does not preclude seeing it as something else at some other time. Conceptual patterns can and do change and ignoring such a possibility leads down the road of myth. Newtonians saw the world as a collection of solid, impenetrable corpuscles related to one another by Newton's laws of motion which presume mass, length, and time as absolutes. Reformed and neo-orthodox theologians have tended to *see* the world *as* the creation of a transcendent God, wholly apart from the world, who demands righteousness from a sinful man. Other theologians have stressed a picture depicting God as immanent in the world with man capable of imitating the goodness of God manifested in the life of Jesus.

Imagination is required when one claims to see the world as something other than its obvious character. This imaginative act forms the basis of theory construction for the presumption of a root-metaphor is the foundation of a theory. But theories are rarely built in an axiomatic fashion starting with the root-metaphor and then adding appropriate categories and laws. Usually the theory is well under way systematizing available data when the implicit root-metaphor underlying the theory is recognized. At

7. Wittgenstein, *Philosophical Investigations*, pts. II, XI; cf. also Virgil Aldrich, "Pictorial Meaning, Picture-Thinking and Wittgenstein's Theory of Aspects," *Mind*, 67 (Jan., 1958), 70–79, and his "Visual Metaphor," *Journal of Aesthetic Education*, 2 (Jan., 1968), 73–86.

this point, researchers and theologians realize that they have been "seeing" the world in a special way in the construction of their theory. The recognition of the imaginative "seeing as" and hypothetical "as if" qualities of theories will prevent us from the folly of myth. This awareness must remain with the theorist, since the longer that his explanation persists and the more confirmation and acceptance it receives, the more likely he will succumb to believing it to be the true way of conceiving of the world. Or, the root-metaphor may generate a series of categories related to one another by analogy. The eighteenth century belief that the world was a mechanism yielded the primary categories of the solid units of the machine (the corpuscular atoms) and the mathematical relations among these particles. By analogy, what happened to small particles also happened to large aggregates of these same particles. The most abstract features of this theory, the mathematical laws of motion, were assumed to describe the motion of all types and conditions of bodies. Or, the various schema may fit together as parts of an organic whole with higher and lower functions. The evolution of man can be described as a movement from the less complex to the more complex without necessarily implying purpose. And theologians have described the providence of God as having many different kinds of activity, lower and higher.

Not only are conceptual patterns hierarchical, but they are also an organized structure in the process of becoming. We have noted that theories are displaced by newer theories and existing theories are often modified in the face of negative evidence. Piaget has argued that all thought is developmental; children move from one conceptual stage to the next in a developmental fashion.[8] From the association of ideas they progress to a logical stage. Maturation involves movement from one conceptual schema to another. So too in conceptual patterns of explanation growth occurs. Some schema develop into others within the conceptual pattern and thus the entire theory may gradually evolve by internal modifications. As the scientist explores the hypotheses of a theory, the confirmations and the disconfirmations that he finds through experiment often bring him to modify the theory. Or, he may decide to change the theory because he sees a better and simpler way of expressing it. Theolo-

8. Cf. Jean Piaget, *The Origins of Intelligence in Children* (New York: W. W. Norton, 1963); and John H. Flavell, *The Developmental Psychology of Jean Piaget* (New York: Van Nostrand, 1963).

gians also explore the puzzles presented by a particular theory and alter it accordingly. On what grounds is to possible to call the modifications of the schema within a theory developmental? How do we know that there is genuine progress in the evolution of a conceptual pattern? Although no logical guarantee exists that theories do develop positively as they evolve, we can suggest that a theory does progress as it expands its generality, as it improves its coherence, as it resolves inconsistencies, and as it accounts for more negative evidence.

Evolution of conceptual explanations in a hierarchical fashion can be seen in the the recent development of theories about quasars and in the development of the concept of God as a process. "Quasar" is a mnemonic term standing for: "quasi-stellar optical objects identified with discrete radio sources."[9] In radio astronomy until the 1960s most of the known radio sources in the universe had been identified with galaxies. A few intense sources could not be identified with a galaxy and seemed associated with unusually blue starlike objects. The first identification of a quasar came in 1962 when radio source 3C 273 was identified as a stellar object. Subsequent spectral analyses of this and other quasars revealed a remarkably large red-shift, usually an indication of a stellar object moving away from the observer. The red-shifts are so large, however, that the distances of these objects would be incredible. Solutions to this puzzle have been proposed on the basis of contemporary physics and it is here that we observe the hierarchical interpretation. After the initial discovery, theories about quasars have grown as massive theoretical interpretations have been presented to explain these strange phenomena. Since the source of the intense radiant energy of quasars remains unknown, various processes involving subatomic particles are offered and these are accepted or rejected as a whole. The researcher does not take one bit of data about a quasar and add it to another without first seeking to integrate it into a known causal explanation. Or, he may modify a known theory slightly before applying it to his unexplained data. The hierarchy arises from the series of known scientific theories applied to the unexplained quasars.

Theologians who have adopted Whitehead's metaphysical notion of a dipolar God possessing a finite pole and a transcendent pole have dealt

9. Cf. F. D. Kahn and H. P. Palmer, *Quasars* (Cambridge: Harvard University Press, 1968).

with a number of internal problems in this concept by a series of reformulations that bring with them a host of other assumptions beyond what Whitehead envisioned.[10] Those who reinterpret Whitehead's God as a "person" present another level of systematic explanation that includes a different set of philosophical problems, theological doctrines like that of the incarnation, and anthropomorphic reference.

In the cases of both the quasar and the concept of God in process theology, as the explanation evolves later accounts overcome earlier problems. Although they may not ever present perfect solutions, later interpretations and modifications of theories usually represent improvements and often are hierarchical in organization.

Our suggestions that there are certain similarities in the conceptual patterns of explanation used by both scientists and theologians should be taken as no more than an assertion of possibilities for future investigation. The fact that what constitutes an explanation depends upon acceptance of historical vogues within a discipline could be applied to all explanations and not just to science and religion. Similarly, all theories should fulfill the requirements of coherence and the absence of inconsistency. But scientists and theologians can learn a great deal from these characteristics, for where scientists and especially philosophers of science have stressed consistency too vigorously, they have formulated an interpretation of science that was more like logic than it was like the actual proceedings of working scientists. Where theologians have shunned the need for consistency fearing that if the standards of logic were applied to their trade, theology would be demonstrated as an impossibility, they ended up by regaling inconsistency. Scientific theories cannot escape from the fallibility of human judgments; personal and social values do affect decisions to accept or reject a theory and affect decisions on what to select as significant factors pertinent to a particular explanation. Scientists need not move to the opposite extreme of exalting personal prejudices; they should still seek objectivity through testability, but such an effort must always acknowledge that there are personal and social factors that do influence the nature of what constitutes a legitimate explanation. Some

10. Earl R. MacCormac, "Whitehead's God: Categoreally Derived, Reformulated as a 'Person' or Neither?" *International Journal for the Philosophy of Religion*, 3, no. 2 (Summer, 1972).

theologians have emphasized the personal element so much that their theologies run the risk of losing their objectivity altogether. If theologies are to be counted as genuine explanations of human experience, they must have some coherence and testability. While it becomes extremely difficult to describe the nature of rationality, one can claim that a major form of irrationality arises when contradictions are present.

Finding root-metaphors underlying scientific theories and theologies brings us to the awareness that both enterprises are fundamentally hypothetical and that to claim finality for explanations in either is to commit the sin of myth-making. Human knowledge whether scientific or theological is fragile and tentative and dogmatism can creep into any discipline simply through familiarity.

Although there are many similarities among the conceptual patterns of explanation employed by scientists and theologians, the two disciplines are fundamentally different. While science explores the nature of the physical world, theology searches for meaning and purpose in human experience. The degree of objectivity that science possesses far outstrips through its public testability and predictive role the objectivity of theology. Theology is certainly more subjective, but its subjectivity is not so confined to the individual that it cannot find at least a limited expression as a legitimate form of human knowledge. Religious experiences are shared and expressed in meaningful language; neither verification nor falsification qualify as tests of meaning that eliminate religious language as nonsense for if they did, they would disqualify scientific language as well. The ultimate feelings and values that men hold can be debated and discussed in a meaningful way. To object that such emotions are limited to subjectivity fails to recognize that human experience beyond perception can confirm hypothetical statements about the nature of life. Explaining the confirmation of theoretical statements, whether scientific or theological, becomes extremely difficult and complex because the observation statement or the experiential statement may be loaded by the proposed theory and one never knows just how many instances are enough to count as a confirmation. Sometimes, one does not know exactly what has been confirmed or disconfirmed. Both scientific theories and theologies are accepted in the face of negative evidence. In the mind of the holder of a theory or a religious believer, however, enough evidence has been presented either of an objective or an experiential nature to justify holding the theory or theology. Decisions about the adequacy of a theory or theology and the truth or falsity of some of its statements must be made upon the basis of a careful examination of the explanation itself and the context in which it is understood.

The conclusion of this study is that one cannot reject religious language primarily because of the forms of expressions which it uses. To object to theology on the grounds that it employs metaphors can only be done in ignorance of the similar use by scientists of these devices. Metaphor is a desirable linguistic device used to express and suggest hypotheses for both scientists and theologians. And myth is similarly undesirable for both since it falsely attributes reality to a tentative explanation. No longer should one contrast the poetic and ambiguous language of religion with the concrete and precise language of science. If theology is odd in its use of words, then science is similarly at fault. A corollary to this discovery denies that there are two isolated languages, the language of science and the language of religion. While it makes sense to talk of these two languages in the sense that each discipline has a catalogue of sentences that can be listed in it, both enterprises use the same language, the language of ordinary discourse, and modify it in similar ways to achieve their purposes of suggesting explanations. Whereas science seeks to explain the nature of the empirical world, theology seeks to explain the nature of human experience especially in terms of its relation to value, purpose, and meaning. And both disciplines employ language in similar ways and use conceptual patterns that, although directed towards different ends, have some basic similarities.

Indexes

Index of proper names

Subject index